ALSO BY DR. CAROLYN EDWARDS

Teach Online:
*10 Simple Steps to Get Your Resume Noticed
and Land the Job*

Books to help children learn and navigate life
Illustrated by Gabrielle Liedtke

I Can Be Anything I Dream

Fun With Money

I Look Good
I Feel Good
I Am Good

The Woman's Guide to Love, Peace and Happiness

Dr. Carolyn Edwards

with Rev. Dr. Dawn Carey on Prayer

Dr. E Empowering You books may be ordered through booksellers or by contacting:

Dr. Carolyn Edwards
dre@drcarolynedwards.com
www.drcarolynedwards.com
1-(786) 309-1773

Because of the dynamic nature of the Internet, any web addresses or links contained in this book may have changed since publication and may no longer be valid. The views expressed in this work are solely those of the author and do not necessarily reflect the views of the publisher, and the publisher hereby disclaims any responsibility for them.

The author of this book does not dispense medical advice or prescribe the use of any technique as a form of treatment for physical, emotional, or medical problems without the advice of a physician, either directly or indirectly. The intent of the author is only to offer information of a general nature to help you in your quest for emotional and spiritual well-being. In the event you use any of the information in this book for yourself, which is your constitutional right, the author and the publisher assume no responsibility for your actions.

ISBN: 978-0-9727040-6-9(sc)
ISBN: 978-0-9727040-7-6 (e)

Printed in the United States of America

For my son Jeremiah, may you always feel love, be love and live life to the fullest. You are smarter and more powerful than you realize!

Acknowledgements

I would like to thank God for my life, the journey and the vision to write this book. As they say, a journey of a thousand miles begins with one step. Each step has been a labor of love.

To all the women that contributed their stories, thank you for your courage, openness and willingness to share in order to help others.

To every female living and deceased, thank you for being a mother, sister, auntie, friend, cousin and girl friend. We could not survive without you.

For every person that dared to believe they could use their power, passion and truth to live life in love, peace and happiness regardless if anyone else believed. Thank you for your strength.

Thank you Rev. Dr. Dawn Carey for being my sister and loving Jeremiah as much as you do. Your family is my family. You have such a big heart. May your assistance with the section on prayer be the key to help women live with faith, trust and an abundance of power.

To my husband for always listening, being in my corner and allowing me to pursue my dreams with passion and enthusiasm. Thank you for helping others believe by taking time to impart wisdom and for allowing me to use your words to live by for the title of this book. We are still waiting on your children's book of the same name.

Contents

Why Am I Here?

*"Before I formed you in the womb I knew
you, before you were born I set you apart."*
—Jeremiah 1:5

*"One needs something to believe in, some-
thing for which one can have whole-hearted
enthusiasm. One needs to feel that one's life has
meaning, that one is needed in this world."*
—Hannah Senesh

One day I sat in my home without any furniture or material possessions and thought life
was over. I was only 30; my father had just
died. I was divorced, suffering from severe migraines,
and unemployed with a new home, a big mortgage, no
furniture and no money in the bank. If you saw me, you
would think that everything in my life was fine. I still
looked good on the outside: my hair was done and my
clothes were sharp because my mother told me, "Never
step out of the house looking a mess and not at your

best," but I could honestly say I neither felt good nor was good with life. I was afraid and had no idea who I was, where I was going or what I would do next. When I no longer had material stuff to define me or my life and no place to go, in the solitude I felt like I had cried many regrets and years full of tears. I stopped thinking about what I no longer had or the negative things I experienced and began to focus my thoughts and energy on what I enjoyed about my life, the people I loved and those that loved me. Then it hit me; I finally realized I was alive, breathing and my life had meaning. I still had so many things that made me grateful. Instead of being mad about not having a job, I used that time to think about my passions and goals. What I realized was I had a purpose for living and talents and skills to share with the world. I found out the external things no longer mattered, that I still had work to do and a vision to manifest. It was time to move to the next chapter in the journey. The information in this book is what I know, what I experienced and what I use every day to live happily, in peace and on purpose. Problems and trials come in our lives to make us stronger, build character and provide the tools necessary for the rest of the ride. As you read the words in this book, know that you are not alone. We all have struggles but you are here for one reason: to live your life's purpose and live it out successfully. You have the power to live your best life fully, abundantly and happily.

Always aim to enjoy the journey, be happy and savor this gift of life. No matter how it looks or how bad the situation feels, you are not an accident. Out of the millions of sperm that could fertilize the egg to produce a baby, you were selected and chosen. That, ladies, is a miraculous event. Every day remember you are special, assigned and appointed to be here for a specific purpose. Let me say it again, you are not an accident. There is no one on this earth like you, with your DNA, that can fulfill your unique purpose exactly as you can; this should make you feel extraordinary. You are more than just a pretty face; you are a fabulous one of a kind creation. As Coco Chanel said, "In order to be irreplaceable one must always be different." We need you and the world needs your gifts and talents. Someone once said, "In a world where you can be anything, be yourself." You are a masterpiece and no one can do it like you can. Delight in doing you. Delight in being you. Do not be afraid to be unusual or special; the world needs your uniqueness.

You only have one life to live and that life should be filled with love, joy, peace, happiness, laughter and purpose. Life has its ups and downs, sunshine and rainy days. Some days have torrential downpours and harrowing winds, but I am here to tell you that in the midst of your storms you can enjoy your life, live it with passion and lots of love. Remember, the best is yet to come. Within you is the power to make your life's journey a tremendously happy ride. The universe would cease to exist without women. We are the only ones that can bring forth life. That is a powerful statement, just think about that for one moment. Sadly, many of us do not know or recognize how powerful we are, so they continue to be depressed, sad, unhappy, overweight, tired, miserable and in the back seat of life as if being driven around in someone else's dream. You can take the wheel and be in the front row, the VIP section of your own life. You have the power to make it happen; you have the power to be happy and live the life of your dreams. It all starts with you. Simone de Beauvoir said, "One is not born, but rather becomes, a woman." The tools in this book can help you use your power to be the woman you have always dreamed you could be.

Have you ever wondered how some people overcome seemingly insurmountable odds and terrible experiences and still live life fully? Have you ever heard stories of people that were homeless, poor, abused, suffering with disease, addicted to drugs or lost, who then turned their lives around to become college educated, multi-millionaires, entrepreneurs, sober and now helping others? What makes them strong enough to not give up and succumb to depression, suicide and continued bad choices? It's simple; six practical principles of living gets them to the other side every time. Happiness is about taking action from the inside out to live fully! It is not just about being rich but being wealthy in all aspects of your life. I am sure we have all met someone or seen someone on television that is rich with money, designer clothes and accessories but has no joy, peace or happiness in their lives. As you read on, you should realize the quality of your life does not depend on the amount of possessions you have. The goal of this book is to help you be happy with your life, all of it. The six principles are based on research, experience, learning, personal fortitude and years of coaching, counseling, praying and action.

Women take on the burdens of the world. We are mothers, sisters, caregivers, company presidents, selfless friends, employees and confidants all while suffering in silence, not enjoying our lives. We wait in vain for a certain day to come before we are happy. Some say I will be happy when I retire, get married, lose ten pounds, move, buy a dream home, the kids graduate college, etc, etc. and the list goes on and on. We dress up the outside with makeup, wigs, weaves, extensions, fake nails and designer clothing to pretend that we are all right. We have become professional pretenders and experts at not addressing our issues. Through years of teaching, coaching and living I continue to see women with forced smiles and no light in their eyes because they are hurting, hiding and pretending that they do not have challenges, hurts, pains, betrayals and some months with more days than they have money. Believe me, I have been there.

We have suffered in silence while we struggled, fell down and had setbacks, but we continue to stretch ourselves, persevere, rise and thrive in the midst of all the negative situations and circumstances. Let every story, every word and every tool inspire you to love and be kind to yourself as well as honor your greatness. You ask, why women? We have been told that we were meant to suffer from the beginning pages of the Bible when Eve ate the forbidden fruit from the tree; however, Adam played a part in that story too, but many continue to focus on the belief that women should suffer and not enjoy their lives. This is absolutely not the case. We are on this earth for a limited amount of time, so why not enjoy every minute doing work and spending time on things that are meaningful?

In many countries, women are still denied basic human rights over our bodies, our choices and our lives. But even with all these insurmountable obstacles, women still make it happen and succeed while enjoying each day to the fullest. Joan Baez said, "You don't get to choose how you're going to die or when, you can only decide how you're going to live, now." My prayer is that we all learn how to live fully in the now and make the most of every situation, every moment and every day. This book is a testament that we have endured many trials, tribulations and seemingly negative situations that could have had us all on medication, living unhappy and unfulfilled lives, but still we flourish and blossom in the midst of our sadness, sorrow and setbacks. Our stories must be shared to remove the shame, motivate and enlighten as well as inspire other women to do the same. We must be our sisters' keepers and teach others how to learn from every lesson, every experience in life. If you are unhappy, no matter if you live in a 12,000-square-foot home wearing Christian Louboutins or a one-bedroom apartment wearing Keds, you take your unhappiness, stress and discontent everywhere you go. We must be the change we seek.

People who know my journey always ask, "How did you keep going?" "What kept you motivated and believing that you could succeed?" "What kept a smile on your face?" Even when I was unemployed and my money was funny while I was sick without any clothes, shoes, furniture, focus or direction, I always believed something better would happen to me if I just kept believing and moving in the direction of my dreams. Losing all my possessions was a blessing. I stopped sweating the small stuff and remembered I could not take one thing with me when I died. So I figured, might as well stop stressing myself out trying to acquire more stuff and enjoy my life just as it was. You cannot have or be your best when you keep focusing on the worst. The veil must be lifted. Let's end the shame and embarrassment. Our truth must be told so we can help others. Sojourner Truth said, "Truth is powerful and it prevails." The truth can help others live successfully. If the truth be told, when I lost my job I was not mad. At that point I was only going to work to see my friends. When they did not come to work, I would call out sick. When I focused on truth and what made me happy, I changed careers and began teaching and coaching. I wanted to help people live better lives. This brought me joy. Helping people live joyfully while doing work they love excites me. I have had the honor to teach and coach many people to live their dreams and have fun while they are at it. I interviewed and researched the lives of other fabulous, happy women as well as studied the science of success, happiness and joy then combined the information into six simple principles to help you enjoy your life and enjoy it in abundance and harmony.

FREE YOURSELF

I want to show you how to feed your happiness and live a life full of joy and fulfillment. To help by allowing women to express themselves, release the pain and be filled with love, compassion and faith while providing the tools to press on and succeed, thrive and experience joy in the midst of life. We are hurting needlessly, hiding under a shroud of secrecy and shame about the circumstances of our lives. Women are very diverse with many skills, talents and treasures to share, but in order to be our best we must stop comparing, criticizing, hurting and turning our noses up or down at each other. The goal is to allow each word to empower, inspire, motivate and uplift us all for success in life. My mission is to affirm, educate, teach, coach and lend a hand so that women can fulfill their purpose and enjoy their lives while living their dreams. Ladies, we do not have to feed into the images society portrays of women as foul mouthed, back stabbing, fist fighting, low self-esteem, designer addicts that will do anything for a dollar while putting our sisters down in the process.

Let's start being about our business; the business of truth, vision, triumph, love and purpose. When we begin believing in ourselves even though we have issues or negative circumstances and begin to fill up with happiness, joy and peace, the negative will become less prominent and no longer the focus of our thoughts and actions. Ladies, we need you, the world needs you. Know that you can live your dreams. But in order to get on higher ground, you have to let go of the lower-level thinking, lower-level people, places and things that have always kept you down. You are here for a reason and your life has purpose and meaning. When you change and transform your life, you will be able to transform the lives of others.

Delight in life and have joy, peace and happiness that surpass all understanding while you use the tools in this book to thrive in the face of hardship, setbacks and let downs. While you read each word take a breath and breathe in faith while breathing out fear and self-doubt. Breathe in hope and breathe out hopelessness. Breathe in peace and breathe out chaos. Breathe in vision and breathe out discord. Breathe in love while you breathe out negativity. Happiness is a choice. Happiness is attractive. Happiness is joy. Happiness is contagious. Happiness is fabulous. Live each day being happy and in peace. Peace about who you are, peace about what you look like, peace about your goals, peace about your career, peace about your wants, peace about your needs, peace about who is in your circle and peace about every step you take. No more pity parties; no more focusing on what is not working. Now is the time to focus on how we can use our energy, thoughts and actions to live fully. As Audrey Hepburn says, "Nothing is impossible; the word itself says I'm possible." Happiness, love, peace and joy begin with you.

THE JEWELS INSIDE

This is not another self-help book for you to read and let sit on the shelf. This is a book about action and doing what is necessary to live your best life. The book includes a chapter for each principle to help you stay strong and empowered through the storms of life and find peace, joy and fulfillment no matter where you are on the journey to living the life of your dreams. The tools are practical yet effective, tried and proven. Within every chapter is the detail to help you understand why each principle is so important to living successfully. Also included is an inspiring and motivational quote by a woman and Bible verse to help you stay focused as you read, digest and master each principle.

A call to women was sent out for stories of victory and triumph as well as success over obstacles, disappointments, mountains and stumbling blocks while navigating everyday situations that could have been the end for many and me too. The ladies in these pages used the principles, tools and resources in this book to not only overcome, triumph and succeed but also prosper and live with joy, passion and peace. Their courage and unselfishness to share and contribute these stories are purely a blessing for every person that reads this book. Each woman used her life stories and lessons to show us that it is not over. If we still have breath in our bodies, then we still have life to live. The stories let you know that your setbacks can be the setups for your comebacks. Women's true stories of difficulties and disappointments are intermingled in the principles to shed light and empower, inspire and motivate us all to live better, do better and enjoy each day to the fullest.

Detailed in the book are the six principles to help you enjoy your life as a whole and not just focus on external wealth and material possessions as evidence of success. Each principle teaches us that happiness, success, peace and joy begin on the inside. They are:

- Vision
- Love
- Power
- Help
- Trust
- Joy

This book is filled with positive inspirational messages and lessons all communicated by women. Each chapter begins with an encouraging woman's quote and an inspirational Bible verse. At the end of each chapter is a summary you can use to develop action steps and affirmations or positive declarations that help you state that what you want to achieve is actually happening. These positive statements will help propel you onward. You can repeat the affirmations to keep your thoughts focused and positive in the midst of the storm. Affirmations should be repeated several times daily with the intent of achieving your desired result. You can write them down and post them around your home, office, car, or in your purse to help you commit to memory your purpose and impress upon your mind the intentions and goals you plan to achieve. Remember your thoughts are the energy that precedes your actions so keep your thoughts focused on good quality things. There is also space at the end of each chapter to write goals and action steps. Remember, action is the means to make your dreams realities.

Everyone needs help sometimes. As the Bible says in Ecclesiastes 4:9–12, "Two are better than one, because they have a good return for their labor: If either of them falls down, one can help the other up. But pity anyone who falls and has no one to help them up. Also, if two lie down together, they will keep warm. But how can one keep warm alone? Though one may be overpowered, two can defend themselves. A cord of three strands is not quickly broken." Be transparent. What you've been through can help someone else breakthrough their negative thoughts, limitations and low self-esteem. May each word in this book comfort you in knowing you are not alone and that your life is valuable. Allow these principles, every story and resource to be the team that lifts you up, inspires, motivates and assists you to live life successfully.

Yvonne Pierre said, "Use what you've been through as fuel, believe in yourself and be unstoppable!" Use that fuel to help yourself and empower others. Who says women can't get along? They lied!! You must not buy into the stereotype played on many reality shows that depict women in scenes that demonstrate derogatory behavior to make others think all we do is fuss and fight and call each other names. Let the tools in these pages be the means to remind you that you are powerful, fabulous, appointed and worthy to live life fully while doing so with joy and passion.

Reading this book is not enough; you have to be ready and take action. Hold nothing back! Give your all to life and know that everything happens when it is supposed to, in divine order and divine timing. Successful people don't just sit around thinking about the great life they want to have; they take action to make it so. You must do the same. Valorie Burton tweeted, "Happy people are more likely to get raises, get promoted and live longer." Why not choose to be happy and live successfully? When you learn, teach and give back to others so all women may live life fabulously. Trust that you are enough. You no longer have to let other people dictate your happiness. If you want a better life, be a better person. Read, think, learn, grow and act so that your life is what you always dreamed it would be! My desire is that each of your lives be filled with lots of love, peace, light and joy. Ready? Set? Let's look better, feel better and be better together!

VISION

"Where there is no vision, the people perish:
but he that keepeth the law, happy is he."
—PROVERBS 29:18

"When you get into a tight place and everything goes
against you, till it seems as though you could not
hang on a minute longer, never give up then, for that
is just the place and time that the tide will turn."
—HARRIET BEECHER STOWE

Have you ever felt like you are going in circles? That no matter what you do, you cannot seem to make it to the top? Are you missing direction or a way to stay centered and achieve your goals? Do you have a purpose for your life or actually know what you are trying to achieve and why? Or are you just going through life directionless? Moving from problem to problem, crisis to crisis? Have you ever been tired and wanted to give up? We put so much time into everyone and everything else that we have little time to find our own direction and set our own goals. Taking time to establish a personal or life vision statement can keep you on track, focused and confident in achieving your dreams.

WHAT IS A VISION?

A vision statement is a description in three to five sentences that describes what you want for your life at some future time; it details your hopes, dreams and aspirations. The statement helps you understand exactly what it is you want, why you want it and how it will make your life more meaningful. It serves as the road map that keeps you motivated and moving along when things seem darkest or off track. The vision helps you not lose sight of what you want to accomplish and press on toward the goal. It gives you something to focus on when you want to see how far you have come as well as notice the positive actions you have taken and experienced on the road to achieving your dreams. It gives your life meaning and purpose. Your vision helps to spotlight what you want to do, achieve, be and strategically decide those you want to associate with along the way. The vision helps you know where to put your energy, time and actions. Indira Gandhi says, "Happiness is when what you think, what you say, and what you do are in harmony." Discover your vision and purpose then set sail for a journey full of direction, goals, confidence, peace and happiness.

The following definition from timethoughts.com sums it up excellently: "A vision statement is a vivid idealized description of a desired outcome that inspires, energizes, and helps you create a mental picture of your target." Without the vision it is easy to get swayed, pushed or distracted. The lack of vision can allow you to lose focus and get pulled in the wrong direction by people that may not have your best interests at heart nor the best intentions in mind. The vision helps you know who you are and what you are about. Your vision is about you and your story. Your life is just that, yours and you are accountable for making it the best you can. Your purpose is the reason why you are here. As the Bible says in Romans 8:28, "And we know that all things work together for good to those who love God, to those who are called according to His purpose." You are here for a reason. You have a purpose on this earth and a vision to achieve. As long as you have breath in your body, you have something to do.

KIS

I am constantly asked by many how to design the vision. It is not as hard as you think, just keep it simple. Find a quiet space and ask yourself the below questions, then write down the answers. This activity is a brainstorming session where you do not censor your feelings, thoughts or emotions but are willing to remain open to receive all kinds of answers while you jot down ideas. Some even meditate or pray on the questions and then write down what comes to mind. Here are some questions to reflect on:

- What do I really want?
- What am I truly passionate about?
- What are my talents?
- What makes me unique and stand out?
- What are my morals and values?
- If I could do anything in the world as a profession and get paid for it, what would I do?
- Where would I live?
- What would I do if I knew I could not fail?
- What types of people would be in my life like husband, friends, children, coworkers, mentors?
- What specific goals do I want to accomplish this month, this year, in five years, in my lifetime?

After you write the answers to the questions, begin making sentences out of them. Read them several times to notice how they make you feel. If they do not resonate with who you are, revise them. The sentences should make you feel strong, inspired, happy and empowered. You will probably feel some apprehension while doing this exercise because you are now dreaming big. Sometimes as we dream or envision what we want, our subconscious will begin to think negative thoughts to make us believe we cannot have what we say we want or do what we resolve to do. This is just the fear of doing something new and stepping out of your comfort zone. Remember, fear is only – False Evidence Appearing Real. Do not be discouraged. Make sure your values are consistent with the vision. It is easy to stay happy and focused when things are going well, but the vision should inspire, motivate and empower you to stay on track even when you are in the valleys of life. Here is my vision statement as an example:

> "I am a deliverer of empowering products and services that help people live joyfully and fulfill their purpose. I am a wife, mother and educator at my perfect weight embodying faith in God and living a prosperous, healthy, happy, peace-filled life in my dream home near the beach surrounded by people I love. This or something better! And so it is."

I know it is a mouthful but this vision statement is consistent with my morals and values of loving God and spending time with loved ones as well as maintaining a healthy weight (that has been an issue for me in the past) while pursuing my purpose and passion to help others live extraordinary lives. Making money and living well for doing your life's work is not a bad thing, so feel free to put that in your vision if it is important to you. My vision is short enough that I can memorize it or post it on a sticky note in my office, car and even in my purse, as well as meditate on it and visualize it daily.

Set Goals

As you embark on living life joyously and successfully you will feel fear, not that you might but you will. You are doing a new and different thing. Experts agree it takes 21 days to make a new habit stick, and during that time you might panic and want to go back to the old way of doing things since that is what you know and what is comfortable. We all feel fear but your vision is bigger than your fears. Completing my PhD was not easy but it was a goal I set for myself years before. I missed a lot of social and family events as well as sacrificed financially to fund my education. If it was easy, everyone would do it. It felt strange to be back in school after ten years. Believe it or not, I did not get the support I was expecting but I knew in order to fulfill my vision, education was one avenue that would help get me there.

When you set goals initially, you might feel like they are not going to happen, the dream is too big for me, I do not have the required skills or I need more education or experience to make my dreams come true. You do not have to make it happen by yourself, nor do you have to have everything happen for you today. Set specific and timely goals to make your vision come about. Give your energy, actions and time to the vision. Break the vision down into smaller goals. Set daily, weekly, monthly, quarterly and yearly goals. After that, set one fantastically outrageous goal you know will make you grow, stretch and do something different in order to achieve it.

Here are some of my goals. One is to be a NY Times bestselling author and have books and products sold all over the world in at least three different languages. I want to be a bestselling author not because it is prestigious or denotes a lot of money but because when I achieve this goal, I know my books will be read by people all over the world and that the words on each page will help them to live inspired, empowered and joy-filled lives. Another is to appear on national and other internationally syndicated outlets to empower as many people as possible. One more is to have the Jeremiah children books turned into an internationally syndicated cartoon and primary school curriculum to show children that all things are possible. Those are some tremendous goals. I also include short-term goals that can be accomplished within one year like finishing this book, participating in six or more empowerment engagements, adding at least three more life enhancing products to the website store, exercising five days every week and taking at least three vacations. These activities will help me achieve the vision of empowering others to live successfully as well as taking care of myself and family. I focus on what I want to achieve and not waste any time or energy on fear or else I would stop dead in my tracks. I keep on moving, setting smaller goals along the way in preparation for the day the opportunities are present to make each goal come to true.

Be encouraged and patient on the road to achieving your dreams. Stay the course and remain faithful and grateful for each small victory. Doing just one thing each day to move in the direction of achieving your vision can help you achieve it. The actions do not have to be extraordinary. Each step can be something as simple as asking for guidance, sending an email, filling out an application, reading a book, writing a note, taking a walk, attending a lecture, giving a hug or reading this book. Starting slowly and conquering small things helps you gain the confidence to handle the big stuff.

Keep track of your successes. I have a list on my office wall that contains some of the goals I have attained. Each accomplishment keeps me on track and serves as a visual reminder that I have achieved many things. Your list also reminds you not to be afraid and to emulate your past successes. If you did it before, you can do it again. Louise Hay says, "Be willing to take the first step, no matter how small it is. Concentrate on the fact that you are willing to learn. Absolute miracles will happen."

Pursue your vision with passion and step into your destiny, one goal and one action at a time.

Focus

Have you ever committed to do something and then things start to go wrong? Situations and people come into your life that tests your resolve to stay faithful to the promise or goal? It happens to us all. These situations arrive to make sure you really want what you said you wanted. The vision helps you to be steadfast and focused during the ups and downs along the way. The vision helps you decide where you want to focus your energy, your time and with whom. It helps you not waste one second, minute or hour on irrelevant things, or in other words, it helps you center your time, energy, thoughts and talents on activities that align with your dreams and help you design your life the way you want to live it.

Having a clear vision should help you eliminate people, places and things that can move you further instead of closer to manifesting it. The vision is yours. It is not to be shared lightly. Not everyone can see your vision nor support you in it. That is okay. People have their own vision for their lives. Comparing your vision to see how it lines up with others will not work; your vision is just that, yours. First lady Michelle Obama said, "One of the lessons that I grew up with was to always stay true to yourself and never let what somebody else says distract you from your goals. And so when I hear about negative and false attacks, I really don't invest any energy in them, because I know who I am." Keep your thoughts on who you are, what you plan to achieve, where you want go and who you want to go with.

We must focus our mind's energy on what we want to happen, what we want to achieve, and how we want to live. Doing so will help the universe conspire with you to bring the right people, circumstances, and opportunities to propel you forward. Take time each day to meditate on what you want to happen. See yourself having the day you anticipate. The more you focus on the positive and what you want to happen, the faster your life becomes joy filled, peaceful and successful. Have you ever consistently thought something bad would happen? Like I will catch a cold or miss my bus? Then the negative things you thought about actually happened? That is because your thoughts have power and you normally get what you expect. This is why it is so important to use your energy to envision yourself living a happy, joy-filled and awesome life. Paula White says, "Our thoughts become words, words become actions, actions become habits, habits become character and character becomes destiny!" Choose to focus every day on what you want your life to be like, not what you don't.

You can do it. There are tons of stories from women to inspire you to keep going and trust in your vision. Many were caught up in negative situations but turned them around for positive outcomes. This book includes some stories but there are countless others. Ask women how they succeeded. Here are a few that overcame obstacles to turn negatives into positives. Marlee Matlin is a deaf actress. She could have used what some term a disability – not being able to hear – into a lifetime of sadness or despair by focusing her energy on her lack of hearing. Despite her difficulties, she is now a world-renowned actress, activist and academy award winner. J.K. Rowling is a billionaire writer and owner of the Harry Potter franchise, but she used to be a penniless, depressed single mother on welfare. Many women helped to secure the right for us to live freely and put an end to injustice in the world like Harriet Tubman, Rosa Parks, Susan B. Anthony, Ida B. Wells and Coretta Scott King. They all faced insurmountable odds but kept focusing on the vision which inspired them to keep moving forward and change their lives and ours for the better. Focus on what you want to accomplish and continue each day to take action to move towards it.

STOP THE MADNESS

When you have doubts – and you will have them – it is just part of life, go back to your vision. Iyanla Vanzant said, "The vision is what pulls you forward. Without vision you will be stuck in what you know and what you know is what you've already seen. Be willing to do the thing that scares you to bring forth your vision." If the situation, circumstances or conditions will not bring you closer to living the life of your dreams, then do not participate in them. If the people in your life are not in line with where you want to be, let them go. If you have thoughts that do not align with your vision, let them go. If the thoughts you think are not working, let them go. If you are used to hanging in places that do not support your vision, let them go. If you cannot let them go immediately (because they might be loved ones or your place of employment), you can certainly decrease or minimize the amount of time you spend on negative thoughts or situations that do not affirm your vision.

Find new places, friends, activities, jobs or thoughts that encourage you, support you, guide you and propel you in the direction of your life vision. The vision lets you know the best is yet to come. Always surround yourself with people and circumstances that fortify you and thrust you forward. Review your vision often as it serves as a reminder of how far you have come and what you have accomplished thus far. Center each activity and your actions on achieving your vision; this helps you build confidence in staying the course and achieving your dreams. You will and you must get out of your comfort zone. Remember, you want to do a new thing on the road to happiness and life success. You know what has not worked; in order to find out what does work, you must change your behavior. Be open and willing to new discoveries that move you forward. Learn, grow, try it, make adjustments then repeat. This is the winning combination. Here is Helen's story of being open and willing, then finding her true vision.

I always wanted children. I was married for two years when we first started trying. Ten years later, still no children. I knew that was my life's purpose, to love and raise the best children in the world. I spent so many years longing for the children I lost to miscarriage, 5 in all. My husband no longer wanted to try and would not consider adoption. I thought my life was over. I could not focus on all I had because I could only see what I lost and what was missing. Everyone that loved me was concerned about me; they kept telling me to seek counseling, to pray about it. But I did not feel like God was listening, loved me, nor was my friend. I was always an educator and had access to children every day, but I was not happy because I was not a mother. I had never birthed a child. Each time I became pregnant, it never lasted. My children never survived. I spent years struggling and focusing on being a mother.

To be honest I did not see much of a future without children. I stopped trusting in my marriage since I thought I was damaged and so my husband could not love me. I felt I had no value and nothing to offer. My question to God was why are you punishing me? I was always asked to volunteer in the children's church but I never wanted to because I was jealous of all the women that had children. The church leaders kept asking me to volunteer and I had no idea why. One day my husband told me to not feel sorry for myself any longer and volunteer. That they obviously see something in me that fits the needs of the ministry. Give it a try, I just might like it. I liked it so much that I kept volunteering each time they asked. That was over twenty years ago.

Although I never had any biological children, God had a bigger plan for me. I am a mother. I am a mother to over 20 children I have helped over the years through several mentoring programs. I have helped so many children live successfully by tutoring them, listening to them and loving them. That is what a mom does. I have received mother's day cards from many, invitations to graduations, baby showers, weddings and calls on Christmas and Mother's day. If I had my own children I am sure I would not have volunteered those hours to help so many others. I am a mother, a mother of many.

Sometimes the vision you seek is seeking you. Your vision can be your calling or the reason why you are on this earth. As Oprah Winfrey says, "I've come to believe that each of us has a personal calling that's as unique as a fingerprint - and that the best way to succeed is to discover what you love and then find a way to offer it to others in the form of service, working hard, and also allowing the energy of the universe to lead you." Many of us have struggled in an area of our lives and wanted to give up but you can still be happy when the vision does not show up exactly as you planned. Trust that you are here for a reason and your life has purpose even when the vision looks different than you imagined. There is greatness in you and talents you need to share with the world.

If things are not working out as planned, this just might be the time to let go and move on to what is next. Keep moving in the direction of your dreams knowing that everything happens in divine timing and order. You will know when it is time to let go. It normally happens when there is no more passion, peace or joy in the things you are doing. Move on to what is next. Do not wait for validation from others; this is your life. Iyanla Vanzant said, "Your vision is for you; it's not for other's to cosign." I agree 100%. We have a tendency to want validation or confirmation from others that our goals are good, worthwhile or doable. You do not need others to buy in to your dreams and goals; if we did, many of the successful women in the pages of this book would never have achieved theirs. Stop worrying about having others believe in your dreams, goals and desires. What others think or feel about you or your goals are not as important as how you think and feel about them. Keep your thoughts and energy on what you want to accomplish. When you let go of what does not work and does not matter, you have room for the opportunities that await you on the path to joy, happiness and life success.

Things to Remember

1. You are designed for a specific purpose.
2. There is no one like you on this earth that can do what you do, exactly the way you do it.
3. Your vision is the road map to keep you focused, motivated, empowered and on purpose.
4. Happiness begins with taking action. Small steps are just as good as big ones.

Affirmations

- I enjoy life to the fullest.
- Every decision brings me closer to my vision.
- I am a uniquely, divinely created woman on purpose.
- There are no failures; I learn from everything I do.
- All my thoughts are focused on the positive; the best is yet to come.

NOTES

LOVE

"Love Never Fails."
—1 CORINTHIANS 13:8

*"Accustom yourself continually to make many acts
of love, for they enkindle and melt the soul."*
— SAINT TERESA OF AVILA

All we need is love! Do you remember that song? Love not only applies when doing for and giving to others; it also entails loving ourselves and being open to being yourself, exactly who you are designed to be. Do you think a butterfly wants to be a fish or a pig wants to be a bird? Each was designed for a specific reason, created for a specific purpose and so are you. Have you ever been on a plane and listened to the safety demonstration? Airline personnel tell you if the plane is going down to put your oxygen mask on first before you help anyone else, even your own child. This has to happen because you cannot save anyone if you lose consciousness. Life is also like that. Before you can care for and give to others, your energy tank must be full. In order to live your life successfully with passion and joy, you must first learn to love yourself, your uniqueness, your body, mind and spirit. You must learn to accept yourself; to look good, feel good and be good each day.

LOVE YOURSELF

There is no one on this earth like you, that can do what you do, exactly the same way you do it. You are a designer original and the gifts and talents you bring to the world can only be given by you! Mary Dunbar said, "We are each gifted in a unique and important way. It is our privilege and our adventure to discover our own special light." Delight in what makes you unique; have confidence in knowing there is no one on this earth like you. There's nothing like the real thing. We must stop comparing ourselves to others and feeling insecure or inadequate because we think that we don't measure up. You can have role models and mentors as well as aspire to have a great career, marriage, family and life like those you admire; however, you will not be able to do it exactly like they have done it because you are not the same person they are. Your DNA is different and you have not lived the same life they have. You do not know their back story or what it took to get them where they are, and in many cases you would not want to pay the high price they paid to get there. You must find a way to make peace with your gifts and talents then hone them in such a way that you are happy with the outcome.

I know you are wondering, how in the world do I love myself when I am so used to doing for others and putting myself last? How do I love myself when I really don't like myself and the choices I have made? You know what you do; you start with baby steps. Take one step at a time. Today is the first day of the rest of your life. Begin to take time for yourself. Even if it is 15 minutes in the morning before the family wakes or you start your day just to give thanks for being alive. Loving yourself can be something simple like polishing your nails, relaxing while you drink a cup of herbal tea, saying your affirmations, visualizing your goals or clearing out the clutter in your closet.

Loving yourself means honoring the time spent with you. This time must be non-negotiable and uninterrupted. This time must be spent to show yourself that you value you. Take some time to read a book, sit quietly and meditate, learn something new, or do something that honors you. If you have a little extra money, take yourself to see a movie, out to lunch or to the coffee shop just to spend time on you. Do not stop living because someone does not want to do the things you want to do. Take the initiative and do them by yourself. It might seem weird or lonely at first, but you must learn how to be a friend to you. Take time out to do things you love.

Get away for a few minutes or take a ride if you must, but this solitary time is critical. Do not answer the phone, do not get on the computer and do not watch television. Do something different, something interesting and something that is just for you. Romance yourself. The same time and effort you would give to a love interest or best friend, give that to you. When we fall in love we want to talk to that person and see that person as much as possible, and I ask that you take that same passion and enthusiasm you would give to someone else and give it to you. This is not the same as being egotistical or conceited. This time is a loving act to show you how much you mean, how much you are valued and how important you are to the world.

We all want love and to be loved but we must learn how to give that same love to ourselves. For those looking for a significant other, get comfortable romancing yourself so you will know what it feels and looks like. When that right person comes along you can make an informed decision regarding who to allow in your life because you already know what it feels like to be treated special and to be made a priority. When you are in love with your being, you will begin to radiate happiness and peace. Others will want to be around you. Daphne Rose Kingma said, "Becoming acquainted with yourself is a price well worth paying for the love that will really address your needs." When you feel that self-love you will know that you are okay and you do not need the love of anyone else to make you happy. Choose love for yourself in all things. Begin a new and loving relationship with yourself.

Stop comparing yourself to others. Women do it all the time; her breasts are bigger than mine, her legs are shapelier, she has beautiful eyes or great hair and on and on. You have to love what you have. Love everything about you. Do you hear men comparing their skin, smile, feet, legs or arms? Why do we make our looks about competition? Be happy with what you have. You would be surprised at how many people would pay to have the things you dislike, such as full lips, large butts or shapely hips. If you have an area of your body you want to work on, say something positive about it. For example, I have large thighs and always have, but instead of talking about how fat or big they are, I embrace them because they help me swim faster, dance better or run longer. If you want to change something about your body, do it in a way that is loving, not because you think someone else is better.

Each morning thank your body for doing its job. Thank your ears for hearing, your eyes for seeing, your legs for walking, your mouth for talking and your mind for thinking. You have to be able to love your body and the amazing job that it does each day to keep you going in the right direction. For the love of life, my diverse women of color, please stop calling your hair nappy. It is not nappy but actually curly. The curls are just really tight. You can moisturize your hair with water and olive oil to make it softer. Thick, curly hair is fabulous. Love it, embrace it. Do you know how many women with cancer would love to have a head full of hair, no matter the thickness? Use positive terms to denote everything on your body. If you do not love and respect you, how can you expect others to do it?

Look yourself in the mirror and say I love you. Say it again; I love you. Tell yourself positive things like I am smart, I am beautiful, I am happy. My husband always tells people, especially children, "Have confidence and look people in the eye. Before you leave the house tell yourself I look good, I feel good, I am good." Funny thing is my dad used to tell me something similar: "When you talk to people or shake their hands look them in the eye, have confidence." Be accepting and loving of yourself. Even when you feel like you have gone back to your comfortable unfulfilling ways. If you slip up just go right back to saying loving things about you.

Be compassionate with yourself and honor yourself in all things. Honor your thoughts by thinking good things. Doing this will help you develop your love-and-honor muscle. By that I mean the more you love yourself, the easier it will be to choose loving thoughts, loving actions, loving people, places and things that are in your life. Loving yourself will help you stop settling for less than what you want, need and deserve from people, life and yourself. As Janis Joplin says, "Don't compromise yourself. You are all you've got." Realistically it will take practice for many of us to love ourselves unconditionally. Remember, take it one day at a time. When you make a mistake, acknowledge it and say something positive about yourself like I am growing or when I fall, I get back up and keep it moving.

Allow yourself time to heal and grieve if you are unhappy about something. If you have sorrow, hurts or pain, give a voice to them. Allow yourself to release the burden of holding them in. Feel the anger, hurt, sorrow and sadness. Allow it to come to the surface. Feel the pain so you can release it. Holding in secrets, hurts and troubles only continue to wound you, your life and your goals, so make peace with your emotions. I always tell my friends seeking advice about some situation or another to give themselves the same love and compassion they would give to a friend that is going through the same thing. In other words be a best friend to you. You deserve it! Allow yourself one pity day if you need it. If you need to cry, whine or be upset, do it and feel it but for no more than 24 hours. When your sorrow time period or your pity day is up, dust yourself off then get back to loving yourself, being positive and trusting that you are enough. Life is still happening and it does not stop because we get hurt or feel fearful. As Louis Hay says, "Love is the great miracle cure. Loving ourselves works miracles in our lives." Be love, feel love, think love and live your life successfully in happiness, peace and joy.

Love Your Health

R E S P E C T. Aretha Franklin sang it so well. We all need respect but I am not talking about it coming from others; respect begins with you. Respect and honor your body. Feed your body good things; foods that sustain life and that serve as fuel throughout the day. Give your body food that will help you think, act and move in relation to the vision you have for your life. Did you know that food affects your mood whether good or bad? Researchers have shown that what we eat is linked to depression, fatigue and headaches as well as happiness, peace and joy. Food is a culprit in body issues like diabetes, high blood pressure, cancer and obesity, but food is also an asset to help you run faster, think quicker and maintain a healthy weight.

You have the power to make healthy choices that demonstrate love of your mind, body and soul. Cut down on the amount of soda, juice, sweets, breads and junk food you put into your body. You want to fill up on vitamin-rich foods like fruits and vegetables and limit foods like chips, candy and soda. If you want to consume calories, go for the ones that really matter and give you the most bang for your buck like leafy green vegetables and those rich in fiber, vitamins and minerals. If you are thinking vegetable and fruits are too expensive, get some frozen vegetables without the sauces and preservatives then steam or bake them. Do not fill your tank up on empty snack calories. They really have zero nutritional value and after you eat them you feel tired, cranky, and bad tempered or you might want to lie down and go to sleep. Food should make you feel energetic not sluggish.

Doctors recommend several small meals throughout the day to fuel your body constantly and avoid the highs and lows of your blood sugar going up and down. Did you know the food you eat also affects how you look? The vitamins, minerals, protein and fiber in food affect your skin, hair, nails, teeth, eyes, bones and weight. If you want to look good, feel good and be good, you have to eat foods that will help you achieve those goals. The wrong foods can lead to wrinkled skin, gray hair and rotten teeth. Who needs that? We definitely do not want to age earlier than we need to. Have you ever read one of those articles where you have to guess the woman's age? In almost every case where women look ten to twenty years younger than they are, the comments include how eating healthy played a major role in the way they feel and look. Before you reach for Botox or cosmetic surgery to maintain your beauty, eat fruit and vegetables and treat your body right. You only have one body and it is expected to last a life time.

Do you want go through life in a luxury vehicle or one that looks like it needs to be in the junk yard? Do not go through life carrying lots of extra weight. It does not feel good and it is not cute. I can tell when I have gained even two to five pounds. It results in a lot of negative consequences. I am tired and not thinking clearly, not to mention my clothes are tight and make me feel uncomfortable. Not everyone is the same shape, size or body type, but we must love and appreciate the body we have been given. Being healthy is the goal to strive for.

The food we eat also affects the amount of energy we have to do everyday tasks like be productive at work, care for ourselves or families, go grocery shopping or walk the dog. Love your body by giving it food that creates life. I did say this is a book about being happy and living successfully, so I would be lying if I said I do not enjoy a great slice of cake or ice cream every once in a while. But only enjoy the empty calories in moderation. These items should not be a daily habit. Our body works hard to maintain our health and regenerate new cells each day, so give your body the food it needs to work properly, efficiently and effortlessly.

Exercise is extremely important to being happy and living joyfully. Regular physical activity has so many benefits. It helps you to maintain a healthy weight, reduce stress and be more relaxed. It gives you more energy to live fully as well as fight off disease. Exercise can be fun. It can be your new hobby and give you a better outlook on life. I hear so many excuses from women why they do not exercise. I don't have time, I don't have a membership to a gym or I don't know where to start. One thing you must do before you start any exercise program is go see your doctor to make sure you do not have any preexisting conditions that you need to know about. We do preventative maintenance on our homes and cars and we must give that same care and attention to our bodies. Once you receive the okay from your doctor, ask for advice on exercises that are right for you.

Exercise does not have to take hours. Doctors now agree that if you do three 15-minute sessions of exercise it is just as effective as doing the entire 45 minutes at one time. Ladies, please stop using the excuse that, "I can't mess up my hair." Would you rather be sick or dead with a nice hair do or have a healthy and well-functioning body, living life joyously, successfully and full of energy and passion with hair that is vibrant, shiny but maybe not the latest style? I choose healthy every time! You can always wear a wig, a ponytail or buy some hair, but your body is irreplaceable.

Get moving. Movement is good for your heart and your body. It's free. It does not cost anything to take a walk, do some jumping jacks, lunges or bicep curls. You can do squats by acting like you are going to sit down but right before your backside hits the chair, stand back up. You can run in place, skip, jump up and down or dance to your favorite song, play basketball or sports with your kids. It all counts. If you have a rope, clothes line or extension cord, you can jump rope. Tools are not necessary; you can use your own body to run, jump, push up off the floor or dance to create a great workout routine. No gym or special equipment needed. If you like tapes and DVD workouts, check your local library or cable provider for free workouts that you can do.

You should also include strength training in your weekly routine because it helps prevent osteoporosis as well as increase flexibility, bone density and endurance. Strength training can be as easy as putting a can of soup in each arm and lifting them above your head to work your shoulders or lift them up to your breast to work your biceps, the muscle on the front of your arm. You can then lift them behind you to work your triceps, the muscle behind your arm. You can bring them straight out to your sides then bring them together and squeeze at the center to work your chest. You can do this entire set of exercises three times and that will add up to 15 minutes. There is no reason you cannot get some form of exercise daily.

When you begin your exercise routine do not forget to drink water. Our bodies are made up of about 60% water and we need water for many reasons. Not only does water keep us hydrated during exercise; water helps lubricate our joints, regulate our body temperature, keep our skin soft and clear, decrease the risk of strokes and heart attacks, clean the waste from our bodies and provide the energy we need to function. Doctors recommend eight glasses per day. Water is free, abundant and widely available in most countries. Water helps sustain life so drink some every day.

Make sure you include rest in your busy schedule. Your body must rest in order to regenerate the cells needed to keep you moving, thinking and creating. Doctors recommend at least eight uninterrupted hours of sleep per night. However, if this is unrealistic for your life or schedule, try to get in a few short naps during the day, those help too. Sleep allows the body to relax. Exercise, water and the foods you eat affect your ability to have restful sleep. Feed your body well. Foods high in vitamins, minerals, fiber as well as low in fat and sugar will do your body good. Be good to your body and it will be good to you. Here is LaTanya's story of loving herself enough to pay attention to the warning signs and take care of her body.

My name is LaTanya Beard and this is my story. My name has not been changed because I am not afraid of letting anyone know how valuable and important life can be. I have been faced with many challenges in my life, but one in particular changed me forever. September 2011, I was home resting, watching a little television when I noticed a brown spot on my shirt but I didn't pay it much attention because I had been cleaning that day. I assumed it was something that either splashed on me or that I came in contact with. The next day I noticed it again on my shirt and found that brown liquid was seeping from my left breast. I called my GYN and made an appointment. I didn't think it was much because I had already had my yearly mammogram and it was negative.

I quickly got an appointment and went the next day and they took several views and eventually a sample of the cells. About a week went by of me trying not to think about the situation then one day I got the call. I was at work when the doctor called and said, "The biopsy (sample) proved to be cancer. You have breast cancer in your left breast." I was shocked and stunned, but I wasn't upset. I thought to myself, how will I handle this, how will I tell my children and family, how will I go on? Although I tested negative for the BRC1 gene (gene that is used to detect breast cancer risk or family history of breast cancer) I decided to go through a double mastectomy to lower my risk of getting breast cancer in my right breast. So on November 16, 2011, I underwent a successful double mastectomy. That next day, I sent a mass text to all of my friends and family letting them know I had surgery and was fine. A week later, I found out that I would not require any radiation or chemotherapy as the cancer was caught in its very early stages.

I did a lot of praying. I envisioned myself healed. I focused on my future and what I wanted to be doing in 20 years. I tried my best not to discuss cancer or wallow in a depressed state. I put all of my trust into God and doing what it took to make sure I was healthy and my body was healed so that I could be around for many years to come. One thing is for sure, we have a different beginning of this great life, but we all will have the same ending. You only have one body and you have to take care of it.

Thankfully LaTanya paid attention to her body and made her health a priority. But how many more of us put off taking care of our health because we feel like we do not have time, can do it tomorrow or believe I am not sick so there is no need to see a doctor? Loving your health means making sure you see your doctor at least yearly for your feminine wellness exams. You should always know the basics like your weight, blood pressure, cholesterol and glucose levels. If you do not know yours make sure you make an appointment with a physician today. You need to see the doctor at least yearly for your physical, mammogram, pap smear and any other tests to make sure you are a healthy woman. Many organizations offer free women wellness exams. Make sure you do not let another six months pass without one. You deserve the time it takes to be healthy.

Love Your Money

What are your thoughts about money? Do you think negatively about your money like you don't have enough, you don't know how you will pay your bills and there is more month than there is money to cover it? Do you believe money is difficult to come by and you have no idea how to make more of it? Do you say, I am broke, I can't afford it? Conversely, are you a positive thinker when it comes to money? Do you know that you always have enough? There is enough money in the world for you to live the life of your dreams? That you have the skills or can learn what you need to make more? Do you speak words of wealth like I am wealthy, I can afford the things I want and need? In order to attract wealth you must first begin by thinking wealthy thoughts, knowing there is enough money in the world to live successfully.

You have to think and know that there is enough for you to take care of your responsibilities and be happy. The caveat here is that the things you want to buy with money must be based on YOUR vision for life. Comparing yourself and trying to keep up with others will not work. As the saying goes, "Don't try to keep up with the Jonses." Who are the Joneses? They are the people you envy and want what they have or to live their lives. Suze Orman says, "Always purchase less than you can afford." When you buy less than you can afford, there is always room to enjoy life, do and be. You will not be strapped each month by bills and financial obligations to maintain things that do not matter or are not needed. Buying less than you can afford gives you freedom and prevents the stress that continually affects you when trying to make ends meet.

Focus on happiness and having enough. Even when things look bleak, focus your thoughts on being wealthy and having more than enough to take care of your responsibilities and desires. When you keep your mind positive about money, you will receive thoughts and guidance that can help bring more money to you. Wealthy thoughts = wealthy life. How do you begin to think wealthy? Start by reading about wealth and money management strategies. There are television and radio shows dedicated to wealth. Many are recorded and on the internet. Conduct a web search for resources on financial responsibility and money management. The Federal Deposit Insurance Company (FDIC), a government agency that insures our bank deposits, has a great free program called Money Smart that teaches you about money. They also have a version for teens, and if you are looking to help kids learn how to earn, save and share, you should get my book *Fun With Money*.

Make a commitment to go on a financial fast by stopping needless spending and select a period of time where you only spend money on what you need like food, shelter and basic necessities. During this time do not use your credit cards, do not eat out but cook meals at home, make your own coffee and do not buy anything new. Focus on the wealth you currently have and be thankful for it. Save what you are not spending. Every little bit counts. Do not neglect the change lying around the house or money found in the laundry; it all adds up. Always be thankful for the wealth that flows to you. When you can be happy over those small coins, you will be blessed and thankful for the abundance.

Money can come from any source, not just from your job or the work you have to do to get it. When I least expected it, I received money in the mail. A refund from my mortgage company, royalties from my books or even a new client referral have all come unexpectedly. Money flows from all sources; be open to receive. You never know where your next source of funds will come from. Do you have an idea or hobby you can make money doing? Millionaires like B. Smith, Martha Stewart and Rachel Ray all created multimillion-dollar empires from their hobbies of cooking, decorating and creating beautiful lifestyles. Money is a good thing and you are deserving of financial freedom. Find ways to do something you love and make money at it.

Be responsible with your money. Pay yourself first. Save some money each month in a savings or retirement account before spending. Find financial institutions that do not charge fees for accounts or that have low minimum balances. Stores like Walmart, Costco and Sams now offer financial services with little or no fees. Some of you are probably saying, "But there is not enough left over after paying bills to save anything." You have to trust and know that you work hard and deserve to pay yourself something before you give all your money away. Even if you save five, ten or twenty dollars per month, you are letting yourself know that I value myself and the time and effort spent in making this money. Know that there is enough and spend what you have wisely. Here are a few tips to keep you going in the right direction:

1.   Be honest in all of your financial dealings with others

2.   Pay fairly for goods and services

3.   Tip your service staff for a job well done

4.   Give freely to others in need

5.   Pay your bills on time, and

6.   Live within your means

Make sure to balance your books at least weekly. Balance your checkbook to ensure you have enough money to cover your expenditures and properly manage what is left over. When you do this be proud of what you have accomplished. Focus your thoughts on wealth and prosperity in all things. Write yourself a check. Put in an amount that you would like to receive. I once had a dream that I received two million and forty five dollars for book royalties. I printed a blank check (you can find one on the internet), then filled in that amount made payable to myself. I know I will receive it, that amount or something better. Visualize an abundant life full of freedom and wealth.

Do not continually buy items you do not want, need or cannot afford with credit. In many cases you are still paying credit card bills for items years after you bought them but cannot even remember the last time you enjoyed them. Michelle Singletary said, "The borrower is servant to the lender. Watch out or MasterCard will become your master." Before you pull out your credit card to make a purchase, take some time to ask yourself, do I really need it, will this make me happy, will I be happy giving it to someone or will I get a return from this investment? If you cannot answer yes to these questions, do not purchase it. I have a new motto for buying: if I do not really love the item or see long-term happiness from it, I will not buy it. This has helped save me thousands of dollars. I used to have a closet full of items with tags still on them months and years after I purchased them. Before I was disciplined, I used to leave my credit cards at home so I would not spend needlessly. Now I only buy things I need or truly, absolutely love. Items that bring me joy or will truly affect someone in a meaningful way is what I now buy.

Money is energy so allow it to flow into and through your life. If and when you buy something, go home and give something away. Do not let your closets, home and life pile up with things you don't need, don't want and don't use. Keep your life, money and closets clutter free.

If you have not used an item within the last year, give it to someone else to use, sell it online, consign it or donate it to charity. Take the time to find a local charity in your area that provides free clothing to low income, battered, abused or any person that needs a little extra help. I practice what I preach and teach. The other day my five-year-old son told me I had too many purses, that I only needed one and to give the others away to charity. I did just that; gave some away so others can enjoy them. There are a lot of great nonprofit organizations that need your new or gently used clothing and give them to people in need. Organizations like Suited for Change, Dress for Success, Wings for Success, Suited for Success and Bottomless Closet help clothe many people. Keeping your finances and life free from clutter allows more money, peace, love and happiness to flow easily and effortlessly to you.

LOVE OTHERS

Give love, kindness, financial assistance, hope and help to others. Everything you want to receive, you should give first. Give of yourself; do it willingly and with a kind heart. By loving, helping and giving to others, you are telling yourself that I have lots to offer. My cup is full, not half empty. I have time, talents and gifts to share with the world. Now, do not get loving others confused with being super woman. The loving others kind of giving comes when you are rested, on purpose and have taken care of your needs and responsibilities. Remember, love is not just a feeling; it is a choice. We must choose to be love. Love is an attitude that allows our lives to be more gratifying because we no longer constantly focus on our needs, our issues or our problems. Love allows us to increase our openness, compassion and giving which help us feel connected and happy with our lives.

Giving is an act of love. Give 10% of everything! This for many is called tithing. It is stated in the Bible and many of the most successful people in the world will tell you that they are successful because they give not only 10% of their finances but at least 10% of their time and talents to worthy causes. Giving not only helps the recipient but it also helps you feel good about yourself and your life while helping others to live better as well. Have you ever had someone do something for you or give something to you after you fussed about it? The gesture probably did not feel as good when it came from their guilt or reluctance. If you can feel the negativity from someone's gift when you know they did not want to give it, they can also feel the same from you when your heart is not in it. Give cheerfully knowing that whatever you give, it will be given back to you.

We used to sing a song in church during the offering taken from Luke 6:8 "Give, and it will be given to you. A good measure, pressed down, shaken together and running over, will be poured into your lap. For with the measure you use, it will be measured to you." The song goes like this: "Give and I'll give it back to you, Give and I'll give it back to you. Pressed down, shaken together. Running over back in good measure, that's how I'll give it back to you." I love this song because it lets us know that you can be happy in your giving, that you do not have to worry about there being enough to go around. Give what you can from your heart; you never know when your giving will change a life. There are so many natural disasters that have occurred lately like the bombing in Boston, tornadoes in Kansas, flooding in Texas, and earthquakes in Haiti, train crash in Spain as well as the explosions in Bangladesh. All the people and families involved need financial help. Every little bit counts.

Giving love should not consist solely of money or material things. You can show others you love them by spending time with them, giving a hug or paying someone a compliment. There are many studies that show when people have something to love their physical and mental health improves. This is why there are programs to let the elderly adopt pets or children build gardens. Humans have a need to love and feel loved. Instead of thinking about what you are not getting or who is not providing the love you need, take time to give love to someone else without expecting anything in return. There are many nonprofit organizations that need volunteers. You can hold border babies in hospitals, read to children and the elderly as well as work at the animal or battered woman's shelter. You can use your professional skills to tutor others, assist the homeless or serve in the local food kitchen. The list of organizations that need your help is endless. Find ways to give of yourself and help others.

Affirm your sister friends and all the great things they are doing. So often we compare ourselves, complain and speak negatively of each other, but today give another woman a hug, a compliment or some help. Speak kindly and highly of other women, catch them doing something great and do it freely from your heart. If you always expect something in return, then you are not giving; you are conducting a transaction. Live happily while giving what you can freely without worry; your happiness will improve immensely.

Daily I smile and give people hugs, whether it is my son or husband, my friends or acquaintances. Many women just need a hug from another woman to let them know they are not alone and that someone understands. I was not always a hugger. I learned the power of a hug when I was going through my worst times. I had lost my job and all of my material possessions in an apartment fire. When I say I had nothing, I mean nothing. Not any clothes, makeup or even a toothbrush, only what I had on my back. I had to start all over from scratch and that was a very trying time in my life. Whenever I became sad or overwhelmed with the magnitude of it all, I would go see my niece Noelle; she was two at the time. She would give me the biggest and best hugs. I would take her to the park and we would laugh and play. I know her mom thought I was doing her a favor by taking her out of the house, but she was actually showing me love by giving me hugs and allowing me to laugh, play and focus on enjoying life. A little gesture of love goes a long way. When was the last time you told someone you loved them, that you are proud of them, that they are doing a good job or that they matter? When was the last time you gave someone a hug? Tell and show someone each day that they are loved. Love is powerful; love is wonderful; love is happiness.

THINGS TO REMEMBER

1. You are the love you seek; treat yourself lovingly in all things.

2. Your body is deserving of love. Feed and care for it well.

3. Your wealth is a reflection of your choices; spend, save and budget wisely.

4. You get love when you give it. Give at least 10% of your money, time and talents.

AFFIRMATIONS

- I give out love and it is returned to me multiplied.

- Love surrounds me every day in every way.

- Every day is a new opportunity to make a difference in someone's life.

- I am rich beyond my wildest dreams.

- I allow love to flow to me and through me.

Notes:

Power

"For God has not given us a spirit of fear, but
of power and of love and of a sound mind."
—2 TIMOTHY 1:7

"The more you connect to the Power within you,
the more you can be free in all areas of your life."
—LOUISE L. HAY

You are powerful! Let's say it together: I am powerful! You have the power to choose the life you want to live, the thoughts you think and the emotions you feel. It is not about what someone does or does not do to us but how we feel about it that makes it real. You have the power to choose negative thoughts, and feel like a victim of life and people or you can think positive, life-affirming thoughts and learn from each circumstance in life. You have the power to choose happiness, joy, peace and success but the use of choice works both ways. You also have the power to choose lack, limitations, disease and depression. Maeve Greyson said,

"No one has the power to shatter your dreams unless you give it to them." The choice of how you live is in your power.

As discussed in the Vision chapter, it is important to remember you are a designer original. There is no one in this world that has the exact same DNA as you and can do what you do, exactly how you do it. Just knowing this should help you recognize that you are a unique, powerful woman. Challenges will come but you must not let them defeat you. You are the director of your life, the composer of your dreams and the captain of your destiny. Hellen Keller was blind and deaf but she earned a Bachelor's degree and became a world-renowned speaker and author even though she had difficulties, setbacks and challenges. She said, "Your success and happiness lies in you. Resolve to keep happy, and your joy and you shall form an invincible host against difficulties." She knew she had the power to control her own future and so do you.

The choice is always yours. You might not feel confident all the time but just the act of choosing is powerful. The act of making a decision and choosing to select people, employment, situations and circumstances that align with your vision is powerful. Oprah says, "Unless you choose to do great things with it, it makes no difference how much power you have." You only have one life; why not choose to live it purposefully, successfully and joyfully? Walk your journey with clarity, passion, peace, energy and faith that you can have what you say you want.

Ask for It

You designed the vision and set some goals; I am sure you are wondering what to do next. As you take each step in the direction of the life you want to live be sure to ask for what you want and need. Matthew 7:7 of the Bible says, "Ask, and it will be given to you; seek, and you will find; knock, and it will be opened to you." Many of us do not have the life we want because we are afraid to ask for it. The time for being timid is over; you are an adult, speak your truth and stop expecting people to read your mind. Did you know that on average women earn 75 cents for every dollar a man makes even when we are doing the same job with the same level of education and experience? More often than not we make less money because we didn't ask for or negotiate the salary we knew the job warranted. Madonna says, "A lot of people are afraid to say what they want. That's why they don't get what they want." If you want something you need to ask for it, trust and believe you deserve it and will get it.

What is stopping you from asking for a new job, promotion or friends that love and honor you? Ask yourself, what is the worst that could happen? If someone tells you no, that is okay. When you get a no, it is not a bad thing but actually a great thing. No in many instances means not now, not yet, not this person or not this job, but it does not mean that the thing you want will never come to pass. Know that your asking is not in vain. As the saying goes, "Nothing beats a failure but a try." So keep asking and moving in the direction of your dreams. If you don't succeed the first time, ask someone else. When you do your homework before asking, you will increase successful results. Homework means before you ask, make sure the person can actually give you what you want. Seek out people that have the information you need, ask those that want to help you succeed, ask experts in the field or those that have the contacts in their network. For example, asking an optometrist why your tooth hurts is probably pointless. The eye doctor has no idea why your tooth hurts. You are wasting time in the wrong place. For that reason, asking people that have the power to give you what you want increases the likelihood of you getting it.

Think big and ask for the outrageous, the outlandish, or something you never thought you could have; then trust in the process and take those baby steps to make it happen. Ask with confidence and conviction. Ask knowing that what you want to happen is on the way. Your mind, the universe and God are never short of ideas. In the mean time, act as if what you want is here now. Experience life as if everything you want is already here. The perfect mate, the perfect job, the perfect car, the perfect weight, the perfect friends, the perfect living situation are here right now. As some say, "Fake it till you make it" and live your dream every day. Be the things that you seek. If you want more love, then be more loving. If you want a new job, then love the one you have while searching for a new one. If you want to be important, then dress like you are already important. If you want to lose weight, then act like you weigh less and eat less. Do your best and be your best at all times. The more you give to life, the more life will give to you.

Don't just ask for things that satisfy your needs but be willing to help others in return. In your asking let others know how you are willing to help or what you are willing to give in return. Maybe what you want can help you be a better employee, a better boss, a better mom, a better wife, a better neighbor or a better friend. Maybe what you want and need will help you build a business that can make life easier for others. Let the giver know what they will get in return for their gift to you. If they say no, move on and ask the next person that can help. Remember, no can be a good thing. No can be just what you need to move on to the next step in your plan or your life.

SEE IT

Our minds are very active. When the mind gets a picture of what you want to happen, it works on making it so. This works whether you have a negative or positive picture. Your goal should always be to think about things you want to have or happen to you, then act as if you have them. If you want to have a certain job, car, relationship, house or any other thing you endeavor to have, create a picture of it in your mind and think on it day and night. Louise Hay said, "Every day declare for yourself what you want in life. Declare it as though you have it!" See yourself having it and get a clear picture of you enjoying it. For example, if you want to learn a new language, see yourself speaking that language fluently and experience yourself in that country speaking to others in that language. Envision yourself obtaining a better job because you are multi-lingual. Include as much detail as you can imagine in order to bring it to reality.

If you have a hard time visualizing without a physical picture, cut out pictures of what you want to have. Get pictures of the perfect house and all the furniture you want in it. If you want a new job or career, take a picture of yourself in the perfect attire for your dream job and include pictures of the perfect work location. If you want a vacation to the Caribbean, find a picture of a beach with crystal-clear water and tape your picture to it. I actually have a dream board in my office that is on the wall facing my desk and I look at every day. It has pictures of things I want to have in my life at all times like love, family, financial wealth, simplicity, as well as material things like my dream home, the perfect office, custom closets, a new car and new sources of clients and income. These pictures keep me motivated and determined. I even include affirmations to help remind me that my perfect life is already here, to enjoy every moment, to give to others and that happiness is the way.

When completing my PhD, I had ups and downs, trials and tribulations, setbacks and times when I didn't think I could go on, but what I focused my thoughts on was a picture of a PhD Diploma with my name on it in the middle of my dream board. I even had it in my vision statement just six years ago. When the going got tough, I visualized myself walking across the stage at graduation and books printed with Dr. on them since I knew I would author many books. As you achieve your goals, you can revise your dream board and vision to dream even bigger and include new goals, wants and desires.

If a dream board won't work for you, create a dream book. The dream book lets you keep track of your goals and what you want to accomplish on every page. It does not have to be expensive. It can be a photo book or even multiple sheets of paper that you staple together. You can use a separate page for different facets of your life like career, family, money, home, health, spirituality and relationships. The dream begins taking shape as you put the book together by including pictures, affirmations and goals on each page then look at it daily. Include images, words, colors, fabric swatches, mementos or anything that will inspire and empower you to live the life of your dreams. Review and visualize your dreams, goals and mental pictures before you go to bed at night, when you wake up in the morning and several times during the day then watch the magic happen. Here's Karen's story of how she visualized her way to success:

Karen was a former student who became home-less after being put out of the house by her mother. Her mother's live-in boyfriend tried several times to sexually assault her. She told her mother about the various incidents but her mom did not believe her. She stated, "You probably were acting grown and flirting with my boyfriend." Karen was hurt by her mother's lack of support and faith in her as well as choosing the boyfriend over her daughter's own safety.

After she was put out of the house without any place to stay, she found herself living in shelters, abandoned buildings and on friends' couches or floors. Even though she did not have a stable place to live or study nor knew when or where her next meal would come, she carried her books. She studied. She found a way to do her homework whether with a borrowed computer or in the library. At one point we found out she was actually living in the school classrooms.

She shared this story with me one day while having lunch in the break room. I never would have guessed she was going through so much turmoil in her life. Although her situation looked bleak and she did not have the family support she wanted or needed, she never gave up on her dream to graduate college. She told me how she focused on the positive things the instructors told her about believing in herself and trusting she could do great things with her life. She visualized herself every day walking across the stage in her cap and gown receiving her college diploma. She worked odd jobs when she could to make sure she had funds to get back and forth to school. She told me, "Even when I was living in an abandoned building with boarded up windows and doors as well as crack heads and drug dealers, I always envisioned a better life with a career, a home and people that loved me."

Karen believed in her dream even when it looked like it was not going to happen, and I am happy to say she was in our college's first ever graduating class. I asked her at graduation what made her keep going through all the adversity and challenges she faced, and she said, "I didn't focus on the negative things that were happening or that happened. I focused on receiving my college degree and all the doors it would open." You too can visualize a better life, a better today and a better future.

EXPECT IT

Now that you have a vision for your life and have mustered up the courage to ask for what you want, use the vision to move into a position of expectation. When you expect something great to happen, you must start clearing out the mess and clutter to make room to receive it. Setting clear expectations helps you begin living in a way that demonstrates you deserve the best and can let go of the rest. Ask yourself how you want to live, how you want to look, how much you want to weigh, who you want to share your life with, what type of job you want and how you want to be treated by all that you come in contact with. Each answer brings you closer to the life of your dreams as well as allows you to let go of those things that are not in alignment with how you want to live.

We teach others how to treat us by how we treat ourselves. Do you treat yourself with respect? Do you feel worthy to receive the things you say you want for your life? Do you feel good about your looks, your body, your health, your friendships and relationships? The thoughts you have about yourself are powerful attractors that draw people, places and circumstances in your life. Mary Kay Ash of the Mary Kay cosmetics empire says, "Every achievement, big or small, begins in your mind." So get clear on what you want, how you want to be treated and then begin treating yourself that way. Don't live someone's dream for you. I know many times our parents have great intentions when they want us to follow in their footsteps to be a doctor, lawyer, teacher, minister, artist, dancer, businesswoman, etc., but what is the dream you have for yourself? How many times have you heard a friend, sister or co-worker say they took the job because someone else wanted them to be this or do that? How many times have you heard a woman say she got married because that was what her parents or fiancé wanted? This is your life; take time to focus on what you want out of it, then act as if you are in anticipation of receiving it.

Expect the best that life has to offer by releasing the negative, limiting and destructive images of the past. The past is just that, the past and it does not have to dictate your future. Alice Walker said, "The most common way people give up their power is by thinking they don't have any." Do not let old negative, limiting beliefs cloud the vision of the blessing of each day and the light for tomorrow. Use every thought to focus on what you want to achieve. Know that you have the power to get it done. I know this is not always easy because of the negative thoughts, baggage or issues we continually play in our minds that tell us we are not thin enough, pretty enough, wealthy enough or smart enough. But with discipline and focus you can center your mind on the positive and what you expect to accomplish.

You might be asking, "How do you do focus on the positive when the negative keeps playing over and over in my mind?" Anytime you have a negative thought, replace it with something positive. For example, if you think, *I am missing the education needed to land my dream job*, replace that thought with, *every day I take action and I am a step closer to getting my dream job.* If you are focusing on your goals and begin to think, *I am not smart enough*, replace that thought with, *I am doing what it takes to achieve my dreams.* Then go find a book, search the internet or get some other information that can help move you forward. When you keep challenging your negative beliefs and commit to living a joy-filled life by constantly replacing the negative thoughts, words and images with positive expectations, it will become easier to expect the best no matter the circumstances because you know the best is yet to come.

When you get clear and act accordingly, you will begin attracting people that are in alignment with what you want, and those that are not will begin to move out of your life. Getting clear and expecting happiness, success and joy allows you to let go with peace when it is time for people to move out of your life and for you to move on or to the next thing. A quote was tweeted, "Don't let someone who gave up on their dreams talk you out of yours." The people that truly want the best for you will continue to support you and your dreams. Remember, whatever you imagine, work towards and expect, you can have. Getting clear helps you to stop settling for less than what you want. If what shows up is not what you want, getting clear will give you the confidence to keep moving forward until the right person, right opportunity, right job, right home or right thing becomes available. Everything is in your life for a season, a reason or a lifetime. Keep it moving with faith and grace while knowing everything is working out for the best. Think and expect the finest, most abundant joy-filled life you can imagine.

SAY NO - TRY IT

As women we give so much of ourselves to others, to our children, spouses, friends, church, charities and employers. We give the best of ourselves and our time to others, then try to survive on the leftover crumbs. Giving so little to ourselves brings about feelings of resentment, frustration, anger, depression, unhappiness and disease. Many of the activities we say yes to are busyness and we have no business giving our time and energy to them. We over-commit, over-spend and over-tax our minds and bodies doing things that are not in alignment with our vision or what we truly want. We often feel guilty if we even think about saying no and doing something instead that motivates, inspires and empowers us to live our dreams. Some call it being "selfish" but if you are not good and loving to yourself and honor what means most to you, then you won't be able to do that for anyone else. If we want to look good, feel good and be good, we must learn to say no so that we do not overextend ourselves.

To make sure you spend time on what matters most, you must find the courage to say no. Learn to set boundaries and be honest about what you can and cannot do. This is nothing to feel guilty about. It is a loving act of honoring your life and being true to yourself. Saying no is choosing to be adult in your choices then clearly and truthfully giving your best to yourself and others in all situations. Do not be afraid of upsetting people. The people you are afraid of upsetting most likely would have no problem telling you no when they cannot or do not want to commit. Give yourself the same loving consideration.

Saying no is powerful. It gives us permission to spend our time and energy on the activities that will produce the results we want. If you are uncomfortable saying no, begin to think about what important things you want to say yes to. If you want more time with your family, more time to exercise, more time to rest, more time to travel, then you will have to learn to say no to other obligations that would prevent you from spending time doing the things you say are important. Say no with authority. Do not waver when you say no. Keep your resolve. That lets others know that your vision, goals and activities are important.

Learn to say no graciously. You do not have to be mean when saying no. No is a loving gesture since we want to give our best when we say yes and do not want to hurt our important relationships or people by burning bridges. Say no very lovingly and if you want, you can offer an alternative plan. Think about when your child wants too many sweets, you say no lovingly because you care about their health and as an alternative to candy and junk food, you can offer some fruit. If you are worried about no, being or sounding harsh to your loved ones, you can use alternative words like not now, not today, the time is not right or maybe I can find someone else to help you.

We cannot do everything, even if we think we can. I have family, friend, self, business and professional obligations as well as commitments to the schools in which I teach. That leaves little time left for much else, especially things that do not support me or my vision of empowering others. So I prioritize my time, spend it with those I love and participate in causes I believe in like my church, the PTA and early literacy as well as women and girls empowerment programs. Practice saying no to requests, tasks and obligations that do not align with your values or vision; when you do this you will have more quality time and energy to give to the people, things and activities that you value. Saying no helps decrease the energy spent on time stealers and energy vampires that can suck the life and happiness right out of you. Increase your no muscle by limiting time and energy on the unnecessary and delight in your newfound energy, peace, happiness and decreased stress.

Things to Remember

1. You have the power to live the life of your dreams.

2. Ask for what you want and need.

3. Create a visual of what you want to accomplish and then live like it's already here.

4. Honor yourself and your needs by saying no to unnecessary obligations and yes to what matters most.

Affirmations

- I can accomplish anything I set my mind to.
- Every day I see and live my dreams.
- Saying no keeps me happy and on track.
- I am confident and ask for what I need.
- Each day I love my mind, body and spirit.

Notes:

TRUST

"Ask and it will be given to you; seek and you will find; knock and the door will be opened to you."
—MATTHEW 7:7

"Anybody who believes in something without reservation believes that this thing is right and should be, has the stamina to meet obstacles and overcome them."
—GOLDA MEIR

After you take action to bring forth your vision, your life, your purpose and the things that matter, you must believe that you deserve it, that it will all come true or something better will happen for you. You must always trust in the something better part because God can dream a bigger dream for you than you can for yourself. I always wanted to live in a warm and sunny place. I tried unsuccessfully for years to move. I went on interview after interview. South Carolina, North Carolina and several cities in Florida to include Jacksonville, Tampa, Orlando and Daytona

Beach but nothing seemed right. During that same time I was also praying for a husband and children. While nothing seemed to fall into place, I still trusted that whatever was best for my life would happen. Fast forward several years. I got married, pregnant and was teaching all of my classes online so that when my husband found a job in Miami, I did not miss a beat. I never had to find a job and was able to work from home when my son was born. I never imagined it would be this good or work this well. The way it worked out was better than I could have imagined. Valorie Burton said, "God doesn't just answer prayer with a 'Yes.' Sometimes He says, 'No.' Often, He says, 'Wait.' All three are legitimate answers." No matter the answer, trust that it is all working out for your good.

TRUST YOUR GUT

Believe it or not we have feelings, intuition, signs and instincts that are inherent in us that tell us what is right for our lives. Often we do not trust what we know, continually forget about our power and go through life living on someone else's terms following their dreams. We are so used to looking outside of ourselves for answers. There is nothing wrong with getting help along the way; however, a lot of what you need you already know because it is on the inside. You are designed with the tools to identify what is right for your life at the right time. Listen to your body, how it feels when you talk to certain people or discuss certain topics. Do you get a feeling of excitement or dread? Are you energized or depleted? Trust what you feel. Forget what you have been told about how things should be done and do what is right for you.

There is more than one way to get to the end. You do not have to follow anyone else's best way of doing things. I learned this with my husband. I have a ritual of cleaning up the house in a certain order, but since he is a man with his own patterns and ways of doing things, he cleans in a way that makes sense and feels right to him. I do not argue for him to do it my way but say thank you for the house being neat and clean. You have to live your life in a way that feels right to you. Of course we must obey the law, but you should begin to make some decisions based on what feels right, what feels just and what feels ethical. People will tell us intuition is not real but those feelings are real, true and help guide us. As Sylvia Clare says, "There is no such thing as chance. Everything occurs as a result of cause and effect; what you do now will create your own future." As you learn to trust your inner knowing, you build confidence by choosing to spend time with people and in activities as well as professions that you love and that make you happy.

What turns many women away from their intuition or knowing is that they cannot easily or practically explain why they feel a certain way or why they made a particular decision. Sometimes we may not know why we feel a certain way until later. Here is a great example. I was introduced to a co-worker years ago and I had a bad feeling about him. I did not want to be around him. I could not explain why because I really did not know him or anything about him. I kept my distance at work. A year later he was arrested by Federal Marshalls for leaking confidential government information. Going with your gut will help you trust what you know and act appropriately. Trusting what you feel can keep you from dangerous situations or circumstances that are a waste of time. You can still make rational decisions by using logic and analyzing them but you should also tap into how you feel about the situation, people, places or things involved.

Have you ever had an urge to call someone or go see someone? You did not know why but this person kept coming into focus and into your thoughts. Did you go with the feeling and call them only for them to say they were going to call you or were thinking about you? Or did you not call then found out they were sick, had an accident or passed away? Have you ever seen someone act in a way you did not like or in a way that did not honor you, your vision or your dreams but you told yourself you did not see what you saw and had to endure something negative or tragic? Maya Angelou says, "When people show you who they are believe them the first time." Trust that you know what to do in any situation. If you ever doubt that you do, you can always pray for guidance. Make conscious decisions and choices knowing even if the situation does not turn out as expected you can learn something from it to use in the future. Check in with yourself when you make little choices and decisions in order to build the confidence and persistence needed to listen to your gut or the voice inside. Give yourself permission to trust that you have everything you need to make the best decisions for your life. Happiness lies within your ability to trust yourself and take action.

No More Drama

Your past does not have to define your future. Just because things did not turn out the way you planned in the past does not mean you cannot do great things now. You can make better choices. Trust that you have the power, will and know how to do things better than you have before. Trust that you can stop negative patterns right now. Today is the first day of the rest of your life and the perfect moment to make it better is right now. You have the power to rewrite your script and remove the drama to make your life a comedy full of happiness, a love story with a happy ending or a documentary with millionaire status. However, you cannot move forward if you keep beating yourself up and letting others beat you up for things that didn't work out in the past. As Iyanla Vanzant says, "Live from the power of your present, not the pain of your past."

Did you know you can change your life and your future generations right now by making new choices? Begin to set a new normal for your life by choosing to make decisions that are based on your vision, love, peace and happiness. You can be anything you want to be. If others have successfully moved beyond the limitations of their past and become great mothers, teachers, entrepreneurs, singers, dancers, astronauts, engineers, beauticians, designers, ambassadors and presidents of nations, you can too. In every crisis there is a message. Susan Taylor said, "Crises are nature's way of forcing change – breaking down old structures, shaking loose negative habits so that something new and better can take their place." Women have been molested, raped, and beaten; they have lost children, limbs and jobs but still survived, thrived and excelled. You can thrive too, no matter what you have been through! Start believing the best is yet to come.

Learn from your past so that you do not have to relive or repeat it. Too often many of us remember more of our setbacks or what we call failures than we do our successes. When negative things happen or our lives do not work out as planned, we often feel very strong emotions. Those negative thoughts and emotions stay present in our minds and get replayed often. Those feelings hold us back from trying again and doing what it takes to live our best lives. If the truth be told, we have all had more triumphs than setbacks and we must start to remember our successes. Start changing your life today by focusing on what you have done right.

When we are teaching our children to walk, talk and write we do not focus on the times they stumbled. We use their successes to keep them motivated and wanting to try again. We tell them to keep trying until they succeed. We have to give ourselves the same loving motivation. I tell my coaching clients to keep a list of their successes for the week, month and year as well as life successes. I post mine on my dream board on the wall in front of my desk and look at them daily. My successes keep me focused on the journey and pressing forward to live my vision and dreams. Your list of accomplishments can do the same for you. Begin writing down each day what you are most happy about and before you know it, you will have a long list of things you did that were correct, amazing and note worthy.

When you are having a bad day, look at your success lists to motivate you to keep moving forward. Barbara de Angelis said, "The more anger you have towards the past you carry in your heart, the less capable you are of loving in the present." In order to be successfully happy, living and loving in the present, you have to learn to take the setbacks and U-turns of life, learn from them, remember the lesson then keep it moving. Every victorious person has had some setbacks and bumps along the way. The bumps in the road let you know what not to do next time. Write down the lessons you have learned and use them to propel you to a brighter tomorrow. Review your success list often to remind yourself that you have done lots of great things and the list is just the beginning of what is to come.

Reward yourself when you achieve a goal. Do something fun, something new and something different. Get a manicure or a pedicure; buy a book or see a movie. The reward does not always have to cost money; it can consist of time that you spend doing something fun, educational, relaxing or soothing like taking time for yourself, sitting in the park enjoying nature, calling a great friend and catching up on each other's lives, polishing your nails or cooking your favorite meal. The reward should be something that keeps you motivated along the journey to achieving your goal or something you look forward to when you achieve it.

It's All Yours

Be accountable for 100% of your life. It's all yours. You are responsible for it ALL. Your vision, your health, your thoughts and your wealth are all your responsibilities. The thoughts you think, the people you share your life with, the work you do, the places you go and the abundance you experience are all based on your choices. Be responsible for it all. No more excuses. You are an adult. You can no longer blame your parents, your upbringing, your genetics, your friends or society. You are the one that has the power to make your life what you want it to be. If you want to lose weight you have to eat healthy and exercise. If you want to have more money in the bank, you have to spend less. If you want to be more attractive, smile more and think positively. If you have emotional or physical issues, seek professional help. If things do not work out the way you planned, be willing to do what it takes to ensure your dreams come true.

This is your life; it is not a dress rehearsal. You have the power to make your life as you want it to be, so be responsible for making it happen. Each day choose to be happy and at peace. Do things you love or that mean something. Choose to act with integrity by saying what you mean and meaning what you say. Trust that your words, feelings and emotions matter. Tell the truth with love but also with conviction. As Pearl Bailey said, "You never find yourself until you face the truth." We must stop living by default which means we must stop allowing ourselves to take what is given and let others choose what is best for us. When you make a decision, sometimes you might have setbacks before you achieve the goal but know that persistence pays off and you are learning what not to do or what to do better the next time. Do not play the victim and blame everyone else for what is not working in your life. Trust that you have the power, wisdom and energy to do what it takes to achieve your dreams and enjoy each day along the way.

Let people know that your words represent truth and honesty. Commit yourself only to do things you know you will follow through on. Do not obligate yourself for activities you do not want to or cannot do. If things change, make sure you call the person in enough time so that alternate arrangements can be made. If you give your word, stand by it. Give people the same courtesy you would want in the same circumstance. Be spotless with your words and make sure the words that come out of your mouth are those you want to represent who you are, your life, your character and your professionalism. This goes for what you say out of your mouth and what you put in writing, whether it is in a text message, the internet or social media. People might not remember what you did for them but they will certainly remember what you did not do or what you said. With all the latest technology people can conduct an internet search and bring back old stuff over and over again. So make sure your words and actions are a true reflection of you and the impression you want to make in the world. If you make a mistake, acknowledge it; there is no failure in that.

Give your truth a voice. The truth will set you free. We must stop silencing our feelings, our concerns and devaluing how we feel. When we hide how we truly feel and do not honor our emotions, we often make bad decisions that delay our dreams. Use your words and communicate them with sincerity. Honesty is the best policy. This does not mean you have to say everything that pops into your head or blurt out words to the detriment of others. Remember, use your words with love and speak life with each one. Speak the truth and trust the process while doing so with the best intentions for everyone concerned. When you use your words do not use them to hurt and harm others; you do not have to belittle someone to make yourself feel good. Do your best not to have an attitude with someone or gossip behind their backs. If something is not working, be willing to stand up for you. Others will not always agree with you but you can agree to disagree and move on. Trust in your power to make the right decision for your life in every situation or circumstance.

Have confidence that you can have what you say you want and think on those things. Your thoughts are the foundation for your life, so stop thinking negative because we normally get what we think about. When you continually think about the negative, you get exactly that, negative. You must choose to think about the life you want to live, the career you want to have, the friends you enjoy and the joy you feel. Trust that whatever you see in your mind you can achieve. I would be lying if I said the optimal situations and circumstances will happen right away. Normally achieving your goals and dreams does not happen overnight, but when you trust the process and keep taking action each day towards your goals, they will manifest sooner than you think.

There are no shortcuts; you know right from wrong, and your spirit and body know too. As Beverly Sills said, "There are no shortcuts to any place worth going." Do the right thing. Even when no one is looking or giving you praise, you know what is right. Doing what is right is good for your soul. Have you ever had someone ask you to take something you know was not yours or falsify some information? When you do not trust you can have what you say you want, this causes many of us to feel we have to take it or cheat our way to the top. If you take shortcuts you probably will only get to enjoy whatever it is for a little while since your conscience will keep reminding you what you did wrong. If it was something illegal, you could even get prosecuted and go to jail. You do not need nor want the stress that comes with operating unethically. When you trust and know you are on the right track, there is no need to lie, steal or cheat your way to get it. The joy is in the doing, taking the action, growing and learning along the way. When you continue to act with honesty, speak the truth and trust in your dreams, you build confidence and strength in saying no to people, events and circumstances that do not align with your vision for your life. This belief in self brings joy, peace and happiness to the process of life.

Never Give Up

Have you ever wondered why some people always come out on top and land on their feet even when things look grim? Did you ever think how some women always manage to have a job even during an economic recession? The ability to believe that you can have what you want is critical to living happily. Even though there are many people in the world that seem like they are doing exactly what you want to do, know that no one on this earth can do it exactly like you can. So keep on moving towards your dreams. Try until you succeed. Take some time to consider those who have been successful and what they did to press on when things looked bleak. Lisa Price, the owner of Carol's Daughter, made her first hair and body products at home as gifts for friends and family. She started small by selling them at flea markets but now her products are sold all over the world. She continued to hang in there when the going got tough and believed in her dream by doing the work in preparation for the day when her products and company would be an international brand.

Oprah continually tells us, "Success is when preparation meets opportunity." When you continually prepare yourself, you are letting the universe and yourself know that you are ready for your opportunity, for your happiness and your dreams to come true. Don't be afraid of possibilities. As Marsh Sinetar says, "Change can either challenge or threaten us. Your beliefs pave your way to success or block you." Trust and believe that the best is coming and your dreams are on the way. When you trust, you are demonstrating faith that you are worthy to receive what you visualized, prayed and asked for and that you are ready to live a fabulously happy, purposed life.

Many times in my life things were not going the way I planned like when I lost my job, my apartment caught on fire or when I had several relationships that did not work out, but I still trusted everything in my life would work out for the best. I continued to do my part in anticipation of my dreams coming true by keeping my résumé current, eating healthy, taking care of my body, reducing stress, enjoying life and being open for the right relationship. When you trust, you know at some point things will happen in your favor; therefore, you must continue to do the work that will prepare you for the opportunity when it arrives.

Some of the world's richest and most successful women like Oprah Winfrey, Spanx creator Sarah Blakely, Zara fashion retailer founder Rosalia Mera, owner of Forever 21 Jin Sook Chang and Gap founder Doris Fisher did not give up on their dreams. They trusted and believed in their products and continued to move forward doing the work to bring their dreams into reality. They did not give up when the going got tough or when things looked like they would not turn out the way they planned. They all were persistent and kept going in the face of setbacks and adversity. You can too. Whatever your dream, whatever you want to accomplish, whatever the life you imagine, trust that you can have it. If you read more about their lives, you will find that they all had faith, a knowing and feeling of trust that they could attain what they wanted. Even though they did not have what they wanted when they first started their business ventures, they trusted in their dream, their vision and their goals so much so that each day they did what it took to move toward the life they wanted to live.

Let Janelle's story inspire you to press on even in the face of detours.

My name is Janelle. I was 17 years old right out of high school when I found out I was pregnant. I was still living at home with my parents and did not know how to tell them or how they would react. My parents were always excited about me going to cosmetology school because doing hair was all I ever talked about since I was about 8 years old. They were both excited about my dream of owning my own salon and beauty spa. I thought about having an abortion since I did not want to disappoint them.

My boyfriend wanted me to have one too but I knew I wanted to have my baby. I was so afraid, I even considered suicide. I felt I had let everyone down but I decided not give up on life. I had the baby and with the support of my mother I was able to enroll in the cosmetology program. My boyfriend did nothing to help with our child but I continued to date him. I thought I was finally on the right track but during the 6th month of cosmetology school I became pregnant with our second child. I so was discouraged, depressed and scared all over again. At age 21, I had two children.

I continually beat myself up about my bad decisions. I was already living at home and had no idea what I would do with another child. I prayed my mother would continue to help because I did not want to give up on the dream of owning my own business or abort my child. This dream was not only for me but for the benefit of my children and family. I already knew where I wanted to open the salon and how many employees I would have. I could put people in the community to work while doing what I loved.

People gossiped about me and said my life was over, that I might as well stop daydreaming because I was a statistic and a disappointment. I tuned out the negative and never gave up hope. I trusted in my dream to become a licensed cosmetologist and to have more opportunities for me and my children. I am happy to say that I eventually graduated and passed the boards to obtain my license. It took a few years more than I expected but I did it. I worked hard and never gave up. I wanted my kids to see me doing something great and let them know that even when things got tough I was willing to study longer and work harder to achieve my dreams. With patience, love, support, faith, belief and trust I opened my first salon. Since then I have opened several more businesses and can now say I love what I do, I am happy and have two wonderful kids. Never give up on your dreams. You have the power to overcome any obstacles if only you believe.

Successful women trust wholeheartedly in their dream to be successful and live the life they envision. Each knows that as they keep working towards it, the work is not in vain. They continue to focus on the goal because they trust it will happen. They do not give up when it seems hard or when trials emerge along the way because they know the work is preparing them for the day their dreams are here. Preparation, determination and persistence show enthusiasm for the dream and the willingness to go the extra mile even when it looks like things will not work out. Detours happen to the best of us but we keep moving towards our goals anyway. Keep on moving while you prepare to receive the finest, the greatest, the most joyous and peace-filled life you can imagine.

THINGS TO REMEMBER

1. Trust that you can have what you say you want, and don't give up.

2. Speak the truth; let your words mean something.

3. Trust your instincts and follow their lead.

4. Focus your time, energy and words on the life you want to live.

Affirmations

- Every choice, thing, circumstance and relationship in my life is working for my benefit.

- Today I conceive. Today I believe. Today I achieve.

- Good things are happening for me. My life is moving in positive directions.

- Whatever I need is on the way.

- I have the power to achieve my dreams.

Notes:

Get Help

"God is our refuge and strength,
A very present help in trouble."
—Psalm 46:1

"I've learned that no matter what
happens, or how bad it seems today, life does
go on, and it will be better tomorrow."
—Maya Angelou

No woman is an island to herself. There is help out there if you just ask for it. You do not have to suffer in silence. Women take on the cares of the world. We listen to our friends' troubles; we solve our children's problems, resolve many work-related issues and think we have to work it all out on our own. Is there something that is bothering you, that you worry about and lose sleep over or something you continually think about? Don't let things you cannot control live rent free in your head. If it is not benefitting you, then get the help you need so you can let it go and move forward into your destiny and live with peace and joy. As Iyanla Vanzant said, "Getting help will help you to choose better, do better and be better."

No More Pain

There are so many tools we can use to release the worry, frustration, depression, anxiety, confusion and negative thoughts we think about constantly. When past problems and situations are currently affecting your right to be happy, know that you do not have to go it alone. Get help. Consider options like counseling, therapy or coaching. Therapy allows you to tell your story to an impartial person that can help you see your life in a more positive manner as well as help you make choices that will lead you in the direction of your vision, goals and dreams. You get a chance to release your feelings in a safe environment where you can explore your thoughts, feelings and situations while gaining understanding. Many health insurance carriers assist with the costs for your mind to be healthy. If you cannot afford to pay for help, there are many free groups for issues like addiction, bereavement, anxiety or health and emotional issues. Many local hospitals offer free support groups. You can find free local services by checking your community directories like the white pages or online directories like yelp.com, yp.com or yellow.com.

Get a mentor. Mentors are people that are doing things you aspire to do or have reached a level of success which you want to attain or emulate. Mentors can provide guidance and insight on how to accomplish what you want. If you look at successful women that enjoy their careers, relationships, families and lives, in most cases they will tell you they had a mentor. Whether a formal mentor or an informal one like a teacher, relative or neighbor, a mentor is someone interested in seeing you achieve your goals. Mentors can help you decrease the time it takes to start living your dreams. They have most likely been where you are and can offer insight on what works or does not work as well as how to move forward. Make a list of people you would like to serve as your mentor. Tell them why you want them to mentor you. Communicate your goals and aspirations. Ask for what you want and need and do not be afraid of no. If they say no, move on to the next person until you are satisfied that you have a mentor that is interested in your success.

Coaching can also be a great source of help. A coach allows you to regain your power by uncovering your wants, needs, goals and vision. Coaches help you take the ideas in your head and develop action steps to make them happen. The coach can help you realize you are the expert and designer of your life and you have the power to overcome any obstacles or negative situations with the right tools. With the coach as a guide you develop a course of action that is best for you. Coaching helps you understand and appreciate the power and authority you have to fulfill your dreams. A coach is your accountability partner to help keep you on track to fulfilling your destiny. They check in with you and help guide you when you veer off course. Coaches can assist you in all facets of your life to include relationships, business, career, personal growth, spirituality and the list goes on. You do not have to do it all by yourself. Trust that you are worth taking the extra steps and get help to move forward in the direction of your dreams.

If you have specific needs with housing, employment, abuse, addiction, health, emotional or other issues, there are many international, national, local, government, nonprofit and spiritual organizations that can help. It is as simple as looking on the internet for an organization that can help with your concerns. Do not let the issues you are having today rob you of your greatness tomorrow. You are worth it. Here is Rose's story:

I was just dipping my toes into the waters of relationships. At age 14 I met a man, and I say man because he was 6 years my senior and little did I know how my life was about to change. The relationship started off very simple and fun but he was overly concerned about the way I dressed and the length of my skirt or shorts. That was just the beginning. A year into the relationship was the first slap; I was in shock. I had never seen or been exposed to domestic violence or abuse and could not believe this was really happening to me. After he slapped me, he would apologize and promise it would never happen again. Of course I believed him.

Time passed, maybe 6–7 months before he hit me again, but it was much more than the slap. The abuse continued; I tried to break it off, but he began threatening to kill me and saying if he couldn't have me, no one else would either. Fear of dying, my pride, shame, youth, doubt, and lack of education about domestic abuse kept me in the relationship. I was able to escape the relationship at 18 once I told my dad about the abuse and sought help. I got a restraining order and looked forward to my future. Finishing high school was a bright spot in the darkness.

The process I used to get out and stay out of domestic violence was being open, telling the truth and seeking help. I encourage parents, especially dads, to talk to their children about relationships and domestic violence. Tell them to know their rights and speak up when people are not treating them right. If they do become involved in an unhealthy relationship, have an escape plan and ask for help.

You do not have to solve each issue by yourself. People really do want to lend a hand and encourage you to make it through. Get the help you need. You can build a great support team to lend a hand along the journey. As Helen Keller said, "Alone we can do so little; together we can do so much." We need you, we need your skills. Your life matters; get the help you need so you can succeed.

KNOWLEDGE IS POWER

There are many resources to assist you on your journey to happiness and living successfully. You can move in the direction of your dreams freely with little to no cost. The information and services are out there. Many are free and available if you take advantage of the opportunities. You can start at the local library. Books can help you learn the skills needed to make your dreams come true. Reading and educating yourself helps you build confidence and self esteem. Reading keeps your brain alive and helps relieve stress. Reading can help take your mind to places you could never imagine. Books give you glimpses into the seemingly impossible. Each page allows your mind to defy time and space, learn about people and places as well as see all you can do and be.

The information found in books can make you more marketable, resourceful and keep you on the right path. Many local libraries provide free employment, tutoring and tax preparation services as well as access to computers with internet and document processing applications. There are books in the library to help you develop an effective résumé, find jobs, learn various languages, increase your health and wellness as well as develop a business. The libraries include newspapers, magazines and periodicals for various interests like fashion, gardening, business, transportation, parenting, health and finance. If you like to listen to authors, many offer free audio books in the library and for download over the internet. You can save the recordings to your favorite listening device and take the information with you. The free opportunities to learn and grow are endless.

Create your own library of resources. Bookmark web page links of helpful sites on your browser page. Buy books that inspire and empower you. Building your library can be little to no cost. Check out yard sales, business liquidations, flea markets as well as local libraries and churches for discount sales on books. In many cases you can find them for 50 cents or less.

Is there a new skill or experience you want to have? Take a class, get the training and attend a seminar or even a webinar on the internet. The internet is abundant with free online training, such as videos on youtube.com and tedtalks.com. Many colleges and universities also post free online courses or seminars. Learning something new gives you insight and a fresh perspective as well as the confidence to try new ideas and skills. You can learn so many great things with just the click of your mouse. Learning gives you options and arms you with the knowledge to make more informed decisions, be more effective and even reach your destiny all while having a passion and zest for life.

Put your tax dollars to work. There are many resources funded by federal, state and local government agencies. Are you out of work? Research unemployment rights in your area. You might be able to get financial assistance, job training or even a scholarship to attend college. Do you need help starting a business? Find online and local business help by checking out the Small Business Administration website sba.gov or calling your local small business partners like colleges, universities, non-profits and local chambers of commerce. If you already own a business many community government agencies provide free grants to help you makeover or innovate your company for business success. When you continue moving forward and trusting help is out there, you will see it appear faster than you can imagine. Be a lifelong learner. There is joy, happiness and power in learning new things.

Write It Down

Journaling or documenting your story, thoughts, hopes and dreams is a great way to let out your emotions on every written page. Writing is cathartic; it's like a hot cup of herbal tea or soup on a cold winter day. A journal is a place where you can clear your mind without fear of reprisal. It's free. All you need is a pen, paper and your honesty. When you speak your truth, you can release stress, worry, doubt and pain of past troubles, mistakes and U-turns. A journal is like a friend that is always there ready to listen and not judge. It is a place to record your feelings, ideas, fears and triumphs as well as give you glimpses of who you are and how far you have come.

Journaling helps you look back and learn from the past. Reading earlier journal entries can help you understand negative things you have gone through, write about each situation, then let it go. When you finish writing about the negative, give yourself time and space to realize what you learned from each circumstance and specify what you will do in the future so that you can move on in peace, love and joy. Writing in a journal can help you realize your power, your strength, your purpose, your destiny and your bliss.

Oprah detailed in her magazine the importance of journaling. She said, *"I wrote a lot of bad poetry in my teens and 20s, mostly about how some guy had done me wrong. I used my journals as therapy. Oh, the time I wasted worrying about men and weight, and what other people thought! In my 40s, I got wiser. I started using journals to express my gratitude—and watched my blessings multiply. What you focus on expands."* Journaling helps you focus your time, energy and efforts on what you want and need and plan to achieve as well as ways to enjoy being happy each moment you are alive.

Years ago when I was laid off and wanted a place to speak freely about the issues in my life, I found journaling was just the friend I needed. I used to go to the park and write down my feelings. I wrote my thoughts and ideas as they came to mind and did not censor them. As a result, I developed the poetry printed on my writing journals. The journals are used daily by people and in support groups, book clubs, training programs, teen groups and church groups to help each person live inspired, empowered and joy-filled lives. You can find them at drcarolynedwards.com/store.

We all have had life-altering events in our lives. Most probably will not happen in the span of a year like they did to me like being laid off, getting divorced, losing all of my worldly possessions in the fire and having health issues when I was suffering with daily migraines. But these seeming tragedies or insurmountable odds turned out to be blessings in disguise. Being still and writing during this time served as a muse to change course and become a teacher, author and move forward with the vision of empowering others to live more freely, joyfully and on purpose. Mary Anne Radmacher said, "Courage doesn't always roar. Sometimes courage is the quiet voice at the end of the day saying, 'I will try again tomorrow.'" Be courageous in your writing and tell the truth so that you can live life with purpose, passion and peace.

Writing in your journal can assist you in being brave while taking the baby steps to propel you forward to live the life of your dreams. There is no correct way to journal. Just write the date and your feelings; it is really very simple. No one gets to see or read your thoughts but you. You can include the vision for your life and goals to help you achieve it. You can include affirmations to help you stay positive as you experience roadblocks along the way. You can check in with yourself to see how far you have come on the road to living the life you imagine and include the things for which you are grateful. Each word in your journal should be a reflection of your truth, your story and help you live life with purpose, authenticity, meaning and gratefulness for every step along the way.

PRAY ABOUT IT (WITH REV. DR. DAWN CAREY)

Merriam-Webster Dictionary defines prayer as "an address (as a petition) to God or a god in word or thought or an earnest request or wish." Prayer is communicating with God, which can be through spoken words, written words, and meditation. After you have asked for what you want and need, pray about it. Your dreams, goals, desires, happiness and destiny depend on it. We cannot do everything ourselves; it is impossible. It is not a sign of weakness to ask for help, guidance, peace, happiness and joy along the way. Talk to God about it, ask God for it, ask God to lead you into it and ask God to surround you with the right people, places and circumstances to help you achieve it.

There is no special way to pray. Like Ruth Bell Graham says, "Pray when you feel like it, for it is a sin to neglect such an opportunity. Pray when you don't feel like it, for it is dangerous to remain in such a condition." You do not have to be on your knees or in a special place, just speak to God like your best friend and hold nothing back. If you want, write a letter to God. Let it all out on the page. Then you can burn it, throw it away or save it somewhere to keep record of all your requests that were fulfilled. Whether you are in the shower, at work, in rush-hour traffic, on the bus, in the bathroom, at the park or even the grocery store, God hears your prayers! So pray. Pray passionately, truthfully and enthusiastically. Talk to Him, trust and tell Him what is on your mind. Release your fears, worries and setbacks knowing that help is always available; you just have to ask for it.

When you pray, do not worry. Praying helps you trust in God and release your fears over the situation. Cast all of your cares on God, knowing that it all will be handled and everything will work out the way it is supposed to. Do not try to control the process, nor the results. Have faith that it will all work out for the best. Paula White tweeted, "Faith takes you from promise to performance!" Keep doing what you know how to do, taking action to move you forward and let God handle the rest. When you pray you have to detach yourself from the how and when it will happen knowing that the Universe will provide. Just keep being happy enjoying your life in anticipation for the best happening for you in every situation. As the Bible states in Philippians 4:6, "Do not be anxious about anything, but in every situation, by prayer and petition, with thanksgiving, present your requests to God."

Say thank you at the end of your prayer knowing that God will provide the best for you. I prayed about moving to a warm and sunny place, and I even wrote a letter about it. I thanked God for it and continued to do what I could do in the meantime. I sent out resumes, went on interviews and even looked at houses in different states. I kept it moving knowing that everything would work out for the best. I prayed the prayer to move five years before it actually happened but I always trusted whatever happened was for the best. When I finally moved, I did not have to look for a new job. I could work from home in Florida just like I did in Maryland. I actually worked the entire time during the transition so I never missed out on any coaching clients or university courses. I never gave up on my dream, even when things got tough and did not look like they would work out. I knew I could always talk to God about my situation.

There might be times in your life when you are sick, physically, mentally or financially. When your entire body aches and words will not come out of your mouth because of the stress you are in. Long well-expressed prayers are beautiful but God answers short three-word prayers too, like "Lord help me." It is as simple as that. When God does it, it is always better than we could ever imagine. No matter how it seems, you always have a place to turn. God is always available no matter the place, time or circumstance. Remember, do what you can and let God handle the rest. Know that you always have help, so use it. Most people think of prayer as a one-way street, a monologue, with only us speaking to God, but prayer should go both ways. Have a conversation with God. Prayer is a time to talk to God, but more importantly, it is a time to be still and listen. Prayer is an exchange. God does not only hear you when you cry out, but He also stays active in your life because God's greatest desire is for you to live life in peace, joy and abundance.

Prayer is our supply line and connection to God but sometimes you might not be as confident in your prayers and need someone to pray with you for what you need. This is a great time to get a prayer partner. This should be someone you trust, believes in your dreams and wants the best for you. I have prayer partners in my life and we pray for each other daily as well as when we have special requests. I also pray special prayers for others or put them on my daily prayer list. Prayer partners help each other grow in faith to trust God with their innermost thoughts and requests. Prayer works and there is strength in numbers. As the Bible says in Mathew 18:20, "For where two or three gather in my name, there am I with them." If you do not already have a prayer partner, you can ask God to help you find one. Many churches have prayer lines.

Search for them on the internet. Let others pray with you for the things you want to accomplish and pray for others in the things they want to accomplish.

A good friend was diagnosed with breast cancer. Doctors told her it was in its advanced stages and there was nothing they could do for her, that she should go home and start putting things in order for her death. Well, she called her prayer partners. We prayed every day for her, her recovery, for the doctors and anyone involved in her care. She decided to get a second opinion and was given two new doctors that conducted surgery and gave her chemotherapy. It took several months of intense treatment but happily, she is now cancer free. She did not give in to the doctors' diagnosis. God has the last say in every situation; talk to Him.

You might be saying this is not a book about God, religion or spirituality, but living happily has a lot to do with trust, faith and believing that you are worthy to be happy, loved and live fabulously while on purpose. You do not have to live depressed, diseased, sad, frustrated or despondent. Prayer and faith are a critical part of not giving up when you are faced with hardships, setbacks, detours, disappointments, trials and tribulations. I can truly say that without prayer and faith I would not have been able to sanely continue going through life after losing everything. Especially when I thought those very things defined me as a person and my value. It was prayer and faith that let me know this too shall pass.

Without furniture or television to distract me, I talked to God. We all have trials but those who live successfully know the valleys are for a reason; we can learn from them and come out on top to live our dreams. Prayer is the vehicle that helps us increase our faith, endurance, anticipation and persistence to keep us moving happily along the journey of life.

Take Your Hands Off the Steering Wheel

Have you ever sat in the back seat and allowed someone to drive you around? When you are not in the driver's seat you have time to savor the ride, take pleasure in the view and enjoy the journey. Allowing others to help can give you time to reflect and maybe get a different outlook or perspective of the situation as well as hopefully a new, useful and positive attitude. Taking your hands off the steering wheel of the situation can allow you to see things through a different set of eyes and hear it through a different set of ears. No two of us are exactly alike. Even if you are a twin you are still different with your own set of experiences. Be open to the good that comes your way; you never know when a diverse perspective is just the ticket to get you back on track to achieving the happiness, joy and peace you seek. Learn how to use your power to look at all angles of a situation knowing that no matter what happens, it is all working out for your good. Humbly accept help and be thankful for it. You do not have to be in command of everything.

Get in a mindset and a position to expect the best no matter what it looks like. Do not worry about it. Live each day to the fullest and keep your thoughts on the positive. Worry causes stress to our bodies mentally and physically. Worrying and stress break us down and can be the cause of headaches, backaches, heartaches and stomachaches. Did you know that 70% percent of the illnesses we have today are due to stress? This is why it is so important to do what you can do and not worry. Worrying causes everything from obesity to anorexia, constipation to diarrhea, and impatience to impotence. Worry can steal our joy and peace of mind. Someone once said, "Worry is a small trickle of fear that meanders through the mind until it cuts a channel into which all other thoughts are drained."

Asking for what you want and need is powerful but relaxing and releasing control by trusting that you do not have to do it all by yourself is just as powerful, if not more. You do know that you don't have to do it all by yourself? Some women act as if they have to be in control of everything all the time. No one knows everything or can do everything. Believe it or not sometimes receiving from others is actually geared towards the giver's needs. In order for others to live fully and on purpose they must give and serve too. In other words receiving allows the giver to also have good returned back to them. Do not be the one that stops someone else from having great things given to them.

If someone wants to lend a hand by cooking you a meal, giving you clothes for your children or even running errands for you, let them. Do not stop them from getting their rewards because you are too stubborn or unwilling to be helped. A good friend is in a women's group that fixes a few weeks of meals for women that have just given birth. I sure wish I was in that group when I had my son. That would have been just what I needed to have one less task on my plate, relax, rest and actually savor the baby and journey just a little more. Getting help allows you to slow down, calm down, spend time in peaceful meditation and contemplation of your next steps. Remember, the helper sometimes needs help and as a result of receiving much needed help, you will be a better helper to others.

Releasing control and being receptive to the kindness of others is an effective expression of trust. Being open and accepting help lets you relax knowing what you need is on the way. When you allow others to assist, you are demonstrating openness to the universe that you are willing to receive as well as trust the process of how and when things will happen. Being receptive to support can be just what you need to stop worrying and learn a new and better way of doing things.

Things to Remember

1. Help is always available.

2. Knowledge is power; be a lifelong learner.

3. Writing it down can help you understand the past and achieve your future.

4. When the going gets tough, pray.

Affirmations

- I am now open to receive goodness and joy every day.

- The help I need is available to me at all times.

- Every day I relax and enjoy my life.

- My prayers are always answered at the right time.

- I am at peace.

Notes:

ENJOY

*"So I commended enjoyment, because a man
has nothing better under the sun than to eat,
drink, and be merry; for this will remain
with him in his labor all the days of his life
which God gives him under the sun."*
—ECCLESIASTES 8:15

*"Success means fulfilling your own dreams, sing-
ing your own song, dancing your own dance,
creating from your heart and enjoying the journey, trusting that whatever happens, it will
be OK. Creating your own adventure!"*
—ELANA LINDQUIST

You only have one life so you might as well get as much joy out of it as possible. Successful people know how to not only work hard but play hard and enjoy the fruits of their labor. You should do the same. There are so many things in life to enjoy along the journey. Putting your mind on your goals and then setting your surroundings for success will help your happiness come faster. Get excited about your life, get excited about your vision, get excited about your goals, get excited about making better choices and get excited about looking good, feeling good and being good each and every day. Your excitement will be infectious and draw the people, places and things to you that will help you achieve your dreams. Life is abundant; there is enough to go around. Do not compare yourself or get jealous of others. You do not know what they have been through to get where they are; therefore, focus on your dreams and the actions needed to help them come true. Maya Angelou said it best, "Life is not measured by the number of breaths we take, but by the moments that take our breath away." Enjoy every minute of your life. Focus on the positive and spend your time, energy and resources on the things that matter most.

Do What You Love

Have you ever heard the saying do what you love and the money will follow? Or do work you love and you will never work a day in your life? You have important work to do. Our lives are happiest when we use the gifts we have been given. Use your talents to do work you love that has meaning and helps others. I have read countless stories of women that were educated and maintained careers in fields like law, medicine, dance, teaching and finance but had no passion for the work, were unhappy and tired of going through the motions for a pay check. Yes, we all must pay our bills and have money to live, but why not make money doing work that inspires, motivates and empowers you to live happily? I am sure many of you are asking, how do I begin to make the change?

Change, happiness, peace and purpose begin with taking action. You cannot just sit around and wait for joy, love and fulfillment to just show up and rain down on you. Start by taking an assessment. Do not base your answers on money, education, skill or experience. Choose based on love, enthusiasm, passion, energy and joy. Ask yourself:

- What do I love to do?
- What do others always compliment me on?
- What activities am I involved in where time seems to fly by?
- What activities would I do for free?
- What do I want to teach and tell others?
- What would I like to leave to the world?
- What in the world would I like to change?
- What matters most in my life?

After you answer these questions create and write your own job description that includes the answers to these questions:

- What type of work do I want to do?

- Do I want to be the boss, employee or entrepreneur?

- Do I want to work for a private company, government or nonprofit entity?

- What hours of work do I like best? Day, night or mid shift?

- Where should I work? Office, home, different country, in nature, on a ship?

- What type of people do I like to work with? CEOs; creative types like artists, dancers or singers; or with more structured types like analysts, engineers, lawyers, doctors, pilots?

Write down your answers in the notes section of this chapter. Do you notice a common theme in the activities you enjoy? What ways can you earn a living doing things that bring you joy? What is stopping you from moving forward? Who can help you get started moving in the direction of your dreams? What actions can you do today to have a job, career and destiny that you love and enjoy? Write it all down and then take action. Be willing to do the work to change your life. Remember, every step counts. Make a phone call, do some research, revise and submit your resume, ask questions. Get moving in the direction of peace, joy and work that you love.

Here are a few stories to keep you motivated along the way. In 1980, Doris Christopher founded The Pampered Chef from her basement in Chicago. She used her experience as a mom and home economics teacher to turn her need for saving time and caring for her family into a business. She developed time-saving kitchen tools and techniques to make cooking quick and easy. Her plan was to take her products to the customer by using sales consultants to give in-home demonstrations on how to use her kitchen equipment and make quick, easy and delicious meals. People could actually try out the products and make meals at the same time. She did not base her business on fear; she knew she loved to cook and wanted to share her tips, tools and resources to help others learn to do it too. Her passion has turned into a multi-million dollar business.

Carol Gardner went through a horrible divorce and ended up in debt but she had a dog she loved named Zelda which was used as the inspiration to start a greeting card line called Zelda Wisdom which is now one of Hallmark's number one sellers. Katrina Parris worked in human resources for over 15 years but when her mother died she realized life was too short. She wanted to do something she really enjoyed. She loved flowers and started small by making flower arrangements but she was so busy with the word of mouth business, she decided to open her own flower shop. There are many stories of women that decided to do something different to stop going through the motions of life and really start living by doing work they love. Ask successful women how they were able to get where they are, and try out some of their tactics to see if they work for you. If you are not ready to make the jump and change your entire career, do what you love as a hobby, as a volunteer, as a friend. Start small. Start by doing what you know. Start by trying it out. Just do it.

Sisters Katherine Kallinis Berman and Sophie Kallinis LaMontagne were in the fashion and finance industries but they had a love of baking which they got from their grandmother at around age eight. They left their high-paying jobs and co-founded Georgetown Cupcake. They started in 2008 with one store but have expanded their business and now have stores in several states as well as a hit show *DC Cupcakes* on the TLC channel. Do what you love because it makes the time go by fast. While I was working on this and all of my books, my husband would have to make me get off the computer. I loved doing the research, I loved doing the writing, and I loved interviewing women for this book. Sometimes I would sit at the computer all day and forget to eat.

My hope is that you love your work so much that you will not realize how much time has passed because it is not work; it's fun, it's love, it's passion, it's joy. Tomorrow is not promised to any of us so why not start doing work you love today? I would be lying if I said it is not scary when you choose to take a different path, a path that speaks to your soul. Not everyone will agree with your decisions but be willing to move forward nonetheless. Half the battle is deciding; the other is showing up ready to do what it takes. As Susan Jeffers writes, "Fear not and choose love and trust when you make decisions." Choose love for yourself as well as love for your customers and clients; then choose to trust the process. It's your life; have fun with it. Nothing beats a failure but a try.

Go First Class

Get in the front seat of your life and treat yourself like a VIP – very important person. No more taking the scraps that life has to offer and being treated as a second class citizen. You are worthy of love, joy, peace and happiness but you have to know it and your behavior must show it. You have to make yourself a priority knowing that you deserve the best. Always do your best and give yourself the best that life has to offer; you deserve it. Go places and do things that bring you joy. Speak positively to yourself, about yourself and others. Positivity is like a muscle: the more you use it, speak it, dream about it, walk in it and believe it, the more you will increase your trust, resolve, resiliency and persistence to go after your dreams. Being positive helps you increase your physical, mental, spiritual and emotional health.

Use your vision to help direct your steps while being a good role model for yourself and others. Let your behavior be classy all the way and only accept those in your personal space that love and honor you. No matter the ups or the downs, make every day a quality experience by being good to yourself and surrounding yourself with positive people that are also good to you and believe in your success. Keep people in your life that love and respect you, that want to see you happy in life and see you achieve your dreams. Someone once said if you want to soar like the eagles you must stop hanging around on the ground with the pigeons. This does not mean to only have people in your life that say yes all the time. We need people that will also say no and check us. We need people that tell us the truth, to challenge us and help us grow. As first lady Michelle Obama says, "In prosperity our friends know us but in adversity we know our friends." Choose to be around people that lift you up. The people you allow in your life should help you stay accountable to your vision and dreams; keep you on track while helping steer you in the right direction as well as share in your joy.

Speak life in every situation; you have the power to learn from every experience. That means use your words to uplift, empower, encourage, motivate and inspire yourself and others. Do not accept the small thinking or negative comments of others, even when they are well meaning family members, friends or co-workers. Remember that you can choose who shares your life and your energy. Hopefully you realize family is not only denoted by blood. As adults we get to create loving families and choose who we spend time with. I learned this by spending years working with various branches of the military. The military life is very transient which means that families move around a lot. Many times families are separated from their loved ones so they learn to build new families and communities of support in each new location. For military people their families consist of the people that love, support and honor them.

You too can create your own family by including people that have your best interests at heart and want to see you succeed, grow and enjoy your life. Minimize the time you spend with people that rob, steal and kill your joy. Do it today. Decrease the amount of time you spend texting, emailing, calling and going places with them. Even if they are parents, siblings or relatives, you have a right to spend your time and energy in places, situations and around people that want the best for you. You don't have to stop loving them but you need to stop letting their negative thoughts, words and actions invade your peace, love and joy.

Live your life with class. When you do something give it your best. Make sure whatever you put your energy towards is a quality project as well as something that will help you live more fully or help others do the same. Show up on time and let your words mean something. If you are constantly late, turn in work that is sloppy, dress as if you do not care about yourself or your life, you will continually meet people that do not respect your time, skills or energy. You might even continue having relationships with those that treat you like they do not care about you or your needs. You have to be the change, the quality and the respect that you want from others. When you are a class act, you will easily recognize people and situations that are not in your best interest then act accordingly. You will no longer feel the need to allow those dwelling in the basement, behaving unethically and unprofessionally to have a role front and center in yours. Going first class is about having an attitude that says I matter, I respect myself, my time and my life and only those that are willing to do the same are allowed to enter.

Get the most out of each moment. Let your light shine, enjoy the journey and have no regrets. I hear many women complain others do not like their personality, their happiness or zest for life. You have to be yourself and live life with passion. There is no joy in shrinking to fit in or make others feel comfortable. When or if you do this you are telling yourself that you are not good enough and your feelings do not matter. Not everyone will like you and that is okay. What is important is that you like yourself. Treat others as you would have them treat you and know that you are a valuable work of art. Not everyone should have a front row seat in your life; some people need to have a seat in the balcony where you can love them from a distance. If someone does not like you or you do not feel like you can be yourself around them, pick some new friends to hang out with or some new places to explore. While you are waiting for the new positive people to arrive, keep loving yourself and doing things you enjoy. Remember, the goal is to enjoy every second and every minute of life.

Let it Go

Stop holding on to old hurts, let downs and setbacks. Forgive yourself for any mistakes you feel you have made thus far in your life and stop blaming people for the parts they played that hurt you. When you forgive yourself and others, you allow yourself to be present in the moment and focus on your happiness, all the great things that are happening and that are on the way. Release the baggage of blaming others for what they did or did not do to get you to where you are right now. They were only doing what they knew how to do. Forgiveness releases you from the past and empowers you to make decisions that are best for you now.

Holding in anger, fear, frustration, guilt and hurt can affect you physically, mentally and spiritually. Physicians show that anger can cause high blood pressure, depression, insomnia, heart attacks, stroke and anxiety. The people that hurt you have gone on with their lives and in most cases are not even thinking about and most likely have forgotten how they wronged you. Do not lose precious moments reliving those hurts. You cannot change other people; you can only change yourself, therefore use your power to let go of the hurts from the past.

Forgiveness in most cases does not happen overnight but you have the power to choose new thoughts, different actions and live life with joy.

You might feel angry at the thought of having to forgive someone that did a horrible thing to you, such as abused you, stole from you, lied on you and cheated on you, but forgiveness is the medicine that allows you to heal and move forward. You must move on with your life so you can get to the happiness, peace and joy that you deserve. Carolyn Osiek said, "It is not 'forgive and forget' as if nothing wrong had ever happened, but 'forgive and go forward,' building on the mistakes of the past and the energy generated by reconciliation to create a new future."

Allow your past hurts to arm you with the power to make fulfilling, fantastic, outrageous, joy-filled and purposeful choices. As Hannah More said, "Forgiveness is the economy of the heart...forgiveness saves the expense of anger, the cost of hatred and the waste of spirits." Anger and hatred waste precious time and energy as well as rob you of realizing your full potential. Ann Landers said, "One of the secrets of a long and fruitful life is to forgive everybody everything every night before you go to bed." When you do this you begin each day with a new slate; you get a new view in which to love and honor your life and live it with joy and passion.

I have clients that are still holding on to old hurts from when they were children. Their sibling called them a bad name, a friend stole their boyfriend, a parent did not let them have something they wanted or a colleague told a lie about them. Do you know these people have moved on and are not thinking about the events you are so angry about which are killing your dreams, happiness and passion for life? By allowing the fear, anger and negativity of the circumstances to stay prominent in your mind, you most likely will think negative thoughts which in turn can make you do something negative or something you will regret. Holding on to negative thoughts and hurts create a negative pattern of fear, distrust and worry in your life, but you have the power to change the harmful thinking and create new and wonderful thoughts, memories and experiences. What happened hurt but choosing to continue to suffer is a choice. Use your power to choose to release the pain, hurt and fear. Do not let it continue to stop you from moving forward.

You can release yourself from past hurts, betrayals and negative situations through forgiveness. It might seem difficult at first but give it a try.

*Say "I forgive '**the person's name**' for doing '**name the event**' to me and how it made me feel; I release the negative thoughts, feelings and emotions and now move on in love and peace for everyone involved.*

By saying this acknowledgement and affirmation of forgiveness you should feel more at peace and the negative thoughts about the situation should no longer be prevalent in your mind, control your mood or your actions. You might need to repeat this practice several times or meditate on this affirmation to truly release the situation. Practice forgiveness whenever you feel stuck and do not seem to be moving forward or achieving your dreams.

Use every situation in your life to build a better today and a brighter tomorrow. If you need help forgiving others, go back to the Get Help chapter. Pray about forgiving others, write about who you need to forgive and seek counseling if need be, but do what it takes to make your life the best. After you do this, be thankful for it all. Everything that has happened to you thus far has brought you to where you are today. As Regina Brett said, "It doesn't matter what has happened to you. What matters is what you do with what has happened to you."

Every event, every person, every job, every hurt, every setback, every pain has led you to today where you can start fresh. Focus on what you do have and not what you are missing. As Oprah says, "If you look at what you have in life, you'll always have more. If you look at what you don't have in life, you'll never have enough." Know that you are enough, learn from what has happened in the past, and use it as the stepping stones to a brighter today and tomorrow.

HAVE FUN

Live life with passion and enthusiasm; why wait until tomorrow? Make every day count. Each day make it a point to have some fun and find a way to laugh. Laughter is good for your entire mind, body and spirit. As some say, you do not need alcohol and drugs to have a good time, laughter is the best medicine. Laughing has a lot of great health properties like boosting your immune system, relieving stress and pumping blood to your heart. It also helps to reduce anxiety, improve your mood and add zest to life. Did you know that laughter is attractive? Have you ever watched someone that frowns a lot and stays angry? That is not an attractive look. I have interviewed many men for some of the Ask Dr. E blog questions and most say when they meet someone what gets their attention immediately is seeing a woman smile, have fun and be approachable.

Laughter lets people see that you know how to enjoy life, avoid taking everything so seriously and can express your fun side. No one wants to date a woman that is always frowning, bitter or negative. Laughter helps you to smile more. Someone once said, "You don't stop laughing because you grow old; you grow old because you stop laughing." Smiling helps you release endorphins that make you feel better and more confident. Simply put, people want to be around others that enjoy life; smile and make the most of each day. Laughing and smiling is contagious and draws people to you. Every day find a way to laugh and smile; you will feel better immediately.

Do things that are entertaining and exciting. Do you like to dance, sing, skate, sail, run, paint or travel? There are so many things you can do that are fun and lots of them are free. Read your local newspaper in print or online to find new and fun things to do in your area. Join like-minded people and get out there and socialize. When I moved to Miami I did not know anyone; however, I am very resourceful so I began searching the internet for things to do. I found a mommy group to have play dates for my son; I found a book club, church as well as professional and social groups. I have found professional colleagues and friends for myself and family by setting my intention and energy on enjoying my life and doing things that matter. Spend each day embracing joy and laughter. Here is Mary's story:

I had been married 25 years when my husband asked for a divorce. I cannot say I was shocked because neither one of us were happy. I know we stayed together for the kids but by the time our youngest finished college I was thoroughly unhappy with my life. I was depressed, overweight and afraid. I just felt like something was missing. I focused so many years on being a wife and mother that I forgot about me and the things I enjoyed about life. I let myself go. I let go of the hopes and dreams I had for myself. Do not get me wrong I loved and still love my children and I enjoyed being a wife but it was time to move on and discover what I was going to do with the rest of my life. I was only 50, still young and very young at heart.

You see I used to be a professional dancer but I stopped dancing when I got married and became a mother. I thought about it here and there but when the marriage was over I needed something to occupy my time. I was tired of going through the motions of rolling out of bed, drinking coffee then watching all the talk and court shows. I lacked purpose and was missing that drive and passion that made me happy throughout the day. I wanted to live, really live. I always wanted to try living in a new city, a different place. I no longer had anything to hold me back.

I moved cross country to California and I started dance classes. I loved all types of dance. I took modern, salsa and even line dancing. I signed up for internet classes and even began learning and enjoying things that I never made time for in the last 25 years. I started to make friends with others in my classes. We would even have lunch and dinner sometimes after class ended. I began to smile more. My kids said they were happy to see me finally enjoying life and that I looked 10 years younger.

With all the dancing, I lost 30 pounds. I joined a travel group and even started dating. Although dating was much different than it was 25 years before, I eventually got the hang of it. At first I thought the divorce was the beginning of the end but it was just a new beginning. I love my life. I even went back to work and started a new career. I now manage a dance studio. I reinvented myself. While I was so focused on what I lost through the divorce, I was missing out on each day, every new discovery and each new adventure. My new motto is nothing beats a failure but a try and if there is anything I want to do, I no longer hesitate. I find a way and do like Nike, "Just do it." Even when things do not turn out the way I expect, I can still see the blessing in being alive. Enjoy each day to the fullest!! I sure do!

I love Mary's zest for life. I love to see those over 50 healthy, confident and enjoying life to the fullest. I look forward to being in the fabulous, fit, fifty club. Dare yourself to try something new or do something you have always wanted to try but were afraid. Have you ever wanted to learn a new language or play a musical instrument? Ever thought about hang gliding, parasailing or jet skiing? Try new restaurants, talk to different people or try new places and activities. Get out of the everyday routine which has prevented you from continuing down the path of personal, professional or life growth and development. Expand your horizons, push yourself and give it a try. Not only will learning something new help make you a more knowledgeable person, it also increases your confidence, trust and openness of life and all it has to offer.

We try new things a lot with our children. We sign them up for various activities like soccer, swimming, basketball, cheerleading, dance, music as well as creative and martial arts but we avoid doing new things ourselves. The same confidence, willingness and openness we expect of our children we should expect from ourselves. We think, *I am too old to do this or that*, but there is no time like the present. Just do it. If you try something and it is not your cup of tea, try something else. Set a goal each week to do something new and different. Variety is the spice of life.

Know that you are never too old to live your dreams. Ernestine Williams is a personal trainer that started weight lifting when she was in her fifties. She is now in her seventies and in the Guinness Book of World Records as the world's oldest body builder. She did not let age deter her from what she wanted to accomplish. She took action by working hard and focusing on her goals. Stop making excuses and start living.

Have fun with color. Use it to your advantage. Color can put you in high spirits. Use it to make you happy, relaxed and inspired. Dress in colors that make you look good and feel good, smile and put your best foot forward. I remember going back to visit family in Washington, DC. My girlfriend and I went shopping in White Flint

Plaza. I kept telling her the clothes are so serious. They are mainly black, blue, tan and grey which to me lack energy and definitely have no pop or pizzazz. I love the colors you find in Miami stores like orange, fuchsia, white, royal blue, yellow and teal. Ladies, we wear white whenever we feel like it, not just before Labor Day. We can find colorful clothing all year around. Our fashions are fun and lively. My other girlfriend puts in her request for bright-colored clothing every year so I can send them to her in North Carolina.

Experiment with color in your living, relaxing and work spaces. Choose shades that inspire, motivate and excite you. Researchers suggest yellows and oranges promote joy and laughter while blues and greens are more calming and soothing. Choose colors that elicit the moods and emotions you want to experience. This is another reason I love living in Miami. Many of the home exteriors are painted in vibrant and exciting shades and hues of diverse colors like yellow, orange, green, purple, pink and blue. It makes for such a thrilling ride as you drive through the various neighborhoods. If you cannot paint the outside of your home in exciting colors, paint your bedroom, living room, kitchen or bathroom. Try various shades; you can always change them if you do not like them. Give it a try; you will be shocked to see how much a small investment in color can change your attitude for the better.

POSITIVE IS THE WAY

Spend your time and energy on things that affirm life and what you want to achieve. Speak positively; believe in your success. Listen to life-affirming television and media. Have you ever listened to negative music or negative shows with a lot of violence? Did you pay attention to how you felt afterwards? These types of activities are low in energy and can make you feel depleted and negative. Strive to view television shows that are positive, enlightening and help you learn and grow. There are many broadcast television and radio shows to choose from. I love the Discovery Channel and HGTV because each time I view those channels, I learn something constructive. I also love *Lifeclass* on OWN. While I am grading student papers I listen to gospel stations over the internet. That music gives me the motivation I need to stay positive and provide students with constructive feedback on their assignments. There are tons of life-affirming free media like self-help books, eBooks, audio books, internet radio shows and podcasts you can access. As Eudora Welty said, "The excursion is the same when you go looking for your sorrow as when you go looking for your joy."

Change your language. Instead of saying something negative, turn it around and state it in the positive. You have the power within you to speak life to your situation and dreams. Use the affirmations in this book to speak encouraging, supportive, caring and inspiring words to yourself and others. People will follow your lead. When you speak positively about yourself and others, you will be surprised that negative people will no longer want to be around you. They will not be able to take all the new and exciting positive energy emanating from you. That is a good thing. It leaves room for helpful, encouraging and positive people to enter. Keep your mind focused on people, places and things that will help you get where you want to be. Dr. Joyce Brothers said, "Success is a state of mind. If you want success, start thinking of yourself as a success." I once heard someone say that you can tell when you are doing great things because people will talk about you. The talking may not always be positive, as they say you might have some haters, but that is okay. If you were not doing something good or noteworthy, people would not be talking about you. Just stay the course and keep living your vision.

Embrace joy, be optimistic and focus on the good in your life. Use your thoughts for things that make you happy, help you grow and help move you in the direction of your dreams. Get back in nature and view life with wonder. Listen to the birds, watch the squirrels or look at fish. They are happy just the way they are doing what they are supposed to do. Each species is designed with everything they need to fulfill their purpose in life and so are you! Try the below exercise to help you to think positively about your life, love yourself, tune out the negative and think encouraging thoughts that help you take action to move forward in love, peace and happiness. When you tune out the negative, you will see that happiness abounds.

Be Positive Exercise

1. For ten minutes each day write every negative thought you have.

2. Make a note of the negative thoughts, words or actions you constantly repeat or that have a recurring theme.

3. Change those listed in number 2 above to positive thoughts, words or statements.

4. Develop an action plan to continue moving forward in patience, love and happiness. For example if you are depressed change your language and develop an affirmation that keeps you thinking positively.

Example Response

1. Negative thoughts - I am fat, I am ugly, things never work out for me, I hate my job.

2. Constant negative thoughts - I am fat, I am ugly, I am stupid, I am always depressed.

3. Develop positive affirming language for negative thoughts -
   - Change "I am fat" to "Every day I love my body, eat healthy and move more."
   - Change "I am ugly" to "I am beautiful inside and out."

- Change "I am stupid" to "I am a lifelong learner living my dreams."
- Change "I am depressed" to "Each day I am happier than the day before."

4. Action Plan – Repeat affirmations daily in the morning, at noon and before bed.

This exercise is about honesty and telling the truth. Do not be afraid. We all have moments of self-doubt but you can only change what you are willing to acknowledge. Even as you begin to enjoy the journey negative thoughts will still come to the surface. Do not dwell on them. Immediately replace them with a positive, loving thought or affirmation. Practice makes perfect. As you continue to think positively you will realize you have more peace, love and happiness than you ever imagined.

Dance like no one is watching. I love the song by Mary Mary "Shackles." They sing, "Take the shackles off my feet so I can dance." What are shackles? Shackles are any person, place or thing that keeps you from living your life fully, on purpose, in peace, love and happiness. Shackles are things, like negative thoughts, low self-esteem, disbelief, criticism, weight, hurt, pain, depression, fear and disappointment, that prevent you from looking good, feeling good and being good each day. Stop letting the shackles of life keep you down. Have you ever turned on the radio and just danced or moved your body to the music and enjoyed yourself? It is so freeing.

You should do this at least once per week. It is good for you, your attitude and your health.

Pursue your dreams with passion and do not let anything or anyone stop you from loving your life. Turn on the music and dance! Move your body, and enjoy your life. Trust you can have what you say you want and do what you believe you can. No special dance moves or rhythm needed. Dance to the beat of your own drum. Enjoy your life, every minute of it.

KEEP IT MOVING

You have work to do so get moving. As Nike says, "Just do it." In order to get your life back and live it with peace, joy and happiness you have to do the work by focusing on enjoying each moment while you keep your vision, goals and dreams ever present in your activities. Take time to decide what you want out of life, then set goals and get moving towards them. Take action to help your dreams along their way, as the Bible says in James 2:20, "Faith without works is dead." What you have done thus far has not worked so do something different, think outside the box or ask for help. The power is in your hands but the choice to live happily on purpose is yours.

Someone once said the definition of insanity is continuing to do what you have done and expecting different results. To put it another way if you keep doing what you have always done, you will keep getting what you have always gotten. If you want to get different results you must do something different. I know you are not insane, so try a new thing. You only live once. Be grateful for it all, even the seeming missteps or mistakes. Every choice has brought you to where you are today and every situation is an experience you can learn from. You can learn from the good and the bad. I always tell my students and clients to be lifelong learners. Be prepared for the joy and be in anticipation of receiving while loving every minute.

Pack light on the journey. Only take what is necessary. Clean out the clutter of your mind, body, spirit and environment. Stock up on life-building foods for your refrigerator like fruits and vegetables. Clean out your closets of any items that you have not worn in the last year. Saving clothes that are old or three to four sizes too small does nothing to bolster your self-esteem. It only reminds you of what you used to be and are no longer. Donate those items to charity and fill your closets, life and home with items that inspire, motivate and affirm the women you are. Getting rid of the old allows room in your life for new to flow in. You cannot receive what is next and new if you keep holding on to what was.

Have you ever known a woman that held on to a relationship that was not working? She kept talking about what and who she wanted in her life but was frustrated because she always had the same tired old experiences? I hear the story all the time. If you want a new relationship you have to release the one that is not working. Do it out of love for yourself. You have to trust that you deserve the best. When you trust, you can open your life up for new, wonderful, loving, happy and joyful people, places, things and experiences. It might seem lonely at first but know you are never alone. Love and happiness are just one step, one prayer or one thought away.

As you navigate your journey be good to yourself and do well to others. Operate ethically and make your words mean something. This helps you sleep at night and brings good back to you. Play, laugh and do things you love; have fun on your walk, be enthusiastic and show up for life. Someone once asked this question: Do you know where the wealthiest people in the world live? Do you? They live in the grave yard because so many people die with their billion-dollar dreams, plans and ideas still in them. They never took the risk or time to share those thoughts with the world. Don't die with your dreams still in you. If there is something you want to do, try it, do it, live it, discover it and tell the world about it.

Get excited about your life, what is happening and what is on the way. There are no shortcuts to doing, living and being well. Happiness, trust, peace, willingness and joy are the way to help you live the life you have always imagined. Use your time and energy on the good and positive things in life. As Erma Bombeck said, "When I stand before God at the end of my life, I would hope that I would not have a single bit of talent left, and could say, 'I used everything you gave me.'" As Harriet Tubman said, "Every great dream begins with a dreamer. Always remember, you have within you the strength, the patience, and the passion to reach for the stars and change the world." It has been my pleasure to share with you the tools to help you live happily and successfully while enjoying each day along the way. May each word in this book, every story of a setback before the comeback, as well as faith, truth and happiness from the inside out be the catalysts for change that allow you to choose better, do better, be better, dream bigger and live happy and successful lives!

THINGS TO REMEMBER

1. Have fun every day; life is to be enjoyed.
2. Let go of fear and negative emotions.
3. Forgiveness will help you to move forward.
4. Keep your life free of clutter.

AFFIRMATIONS

- Every day I love my life.
- Joy floods my thoughts and my life.
- I am open to the good life has to offer.
- I am kind, I am loving, I am happy.
- I look good, I feel good, I am good.

Notes:

Contact Dr. Carolyn Edwards

If you would like information on how Dr. Carolyn Edwards can help you live happily, love what you do and do what you love while living your dreams, go to www.drcarolynedwards.com. There you will find free downloads as well as empowering products to get you moving in the direction of living happily and successfully. Follow Dr. E at www.twitter.com/dreoncall or www.drcarolynedwards.wordpress.com and get tips, tools, resources and inspiration.

If you want further information on coaching and training services, email Dr. Edwards at dre@drcarolynedwards.com or fill out the contact form at www.drcarolynedwards.com/contact.

Rev. Dr. Dawn Carey is a pastor, preacher, teacher, lecturer and advisor. She is the founder of Daybreak Enterprises Inc. an organization dedicated to empowering and enriching others spiritually, mentally as well as their physical well-being. Dr. Dawn Carey uses her life to inspire, empower and motivate people to live their best life. She resides in Miami with her family. You can contact Dr. Dawn at Daybreak91@aol.com, 305-724-4075.

1. There are 6 principles Dr. Edwards shares in order to live with love, peace and happiness which are: Vision, Love, Power, Help, Trust and Joy. Did any of the principles specifically resonate with you? Why or why not?

2. Are you satisfied with the person you are today?

3. If you could change anything about your life what would it be and why?

4. Do you have a vision for your life? If not why?

5. Do you set goals? Why or why not?

6. Are you harboring any old hurts?

7. Is there anyone you need to forgive?

8. Did the true stories relate to you in any way? If not do you know someone that has gone through similar experiences?

9. What insight did you glean from the book?

10. Do you feel the information was easy to read and included all sides of the issue?

11. Do you feel that because men are not included in the target audience that there are some biases that exist in the material?

12. Has the book increased your awareness in any way?

13. Was there a specific passage that left an impression, good or bad? Share the passage and its effect.

14. Do you feel there were any steps to being happy that were not included in the book?

For more information www.drcarolynedwards.com

Send questions or comments www.twitter.com/dreoncall or www.facebook.com/drcarolynedwards

Index